SPIRITUAL
PREPARATION
FOR _____
CHRISTIAN
LEADERSHIP

SPIRITUAL PREPARATION FOR CHRISTIAN LEADERSHIP

E. GLENN HINSON

UPPER ROOM BOOKS
NASHVILLE

The Upper Room Web Site: http://www.upperroom.org

Scripture quotations not otherwise identified are from the New Revised Standard Version of the Bible, © 1989 by the Division of Christian Education of the National Council of the Churches of Christ in the USA. Used by permission.

Scripture quotations identified as AT or AP are the work of the author.

Excerpt from *Hadewijch*, translation and introduction by Mother Columba Hart, O.S.B., © 1980 by The Missionary Society of St. Paul the Apostle in the State of New York. Used by permission of Paulist Press.

Excerpt from "Cantus Amoris" in *Richard Rolle, The English Writings*; translated, edited, and introduced by Rosamund S. Allen. © 1988 by Rosamund S. Allen. Used by permission of Paulist Press.

From "The Canticle of Brother Sun" in *St. Francis of Assisi: Writings and Early Biographies*, edited by Marion A. Habig. Copyright © 1973 by Franciscan Herald Press. Reprinted by permission of the publisher.

Excerpts from *Markings* by Dag Hammarskjöld, trans., Auden/Sjöberg. Translation Copyright © 1964 by Alfred A. Knopf, Inc. and Faber & Faber, Ltd. Reprinted by permission of Alfred A. Knopf, Inc. and Faber & Faber, Ltd., London.

Excerpt from "Birthing an Academy" by Danny E. Morris is used by permission of the author.

Exterior and interior design: Jim Bateman
Photo: David Sacks/FPG International LLC

First printing: September 1999

Library of Congress Cataloging-in-Publication Data

Hinson, E. Glenn
    Spiritual preparation for Christian leadership / E. Glenn Hinson
       p.   cm.
    Includes bibliographical references.
    ISBN 0-8358-0888-2
    1. Clergy--Religious life. 2. Spiritual formation. I. Title.
BV4011.6.H56   1999   98-55759
248.8'92--DC21   CIP

Printed in the United States of America

In Memory of

Fleta and Osse Marsh

Souls like that, one has to have God to
account for them.

—Claude Montefiore in appreciation of
Baron von Hügel

Contents

Preface

1   Is Spiritual Formation Needed?   1

2   Spiritual Formation of Christian Leaders
in History   14

3   The Main Thing: A Relationship with God   36

4   Holding Yourself Accountable   57

5   Making the Most of Your Time   77

6   Maintaining Balance   94

7   Sexuality and Spirituality   117

8   Sustaining the Spiritual Life,
I: Spiritual Reading, Listening, and Seeing   134

9   Sustaining the Spiritual Life, II: Seeking Solitude
and Silence   149

10   Sustaining the Spiritual Life, III: Sharing the
Journey   164

11   What the World and the Church Need Most   180

Appendix: Personality and Spirituality   196

Selected Bibliography   206

Preface

This book is about spiritual preparation for Christian leadership. The word leadership applies to more than ordained professional ministers—pastors, ministers of education or formation, ministers of music, chaplains, counselors, and so forth. It refers as well to the many Christians who play leading roles in the Body of Christ, wherever it extends itself into the world. Open-eyed observation of what goes on in the life of the churches will readily confirm that the ordained supply only a fraction of the leadership needed for the church to carry out the work of the living Christ in the world today.

It doesn't take long hours of study, either, to recognize that a Christian leader needs spiritual preparation. Christian ministry is a difficult, demanding, stressful, costly occupation. The church and the world expect much of a Christian leader. Like it or not, you will be, as the Apostle's word to Timothy (1 Tim. 4:12) charges, a model for believers in word, conduct, love, faithfulness, and purity. So, too, you will be called upon to do far more than the human mind can conceive or human abilities will permit. Who is up to that? Well, the answer is: No one on his or her own resources. Your confidence must rest, rather, just as the Apostle Paul knew so well, not in yourself but in God, who can make you competent to be a minister of this new covenant.

This book is a product of nearly forty years of trying to prepare ministers for their trying task, most of it spent teaching church history at the Southern Baptist Theological Seminary in Louisville, Kentucky. Since 1992, however, I have taught spirituality at Baptist Theological Seminary at Richmond. A shift to another field was not something that I anticipated or planned for myself, but it has turned out to be more or less providential, another of those instances in which life's interruptions turned out to be God's opportunities. At the very least it has helped me to put together and try out much of the material found in this book on bright and energetic candidates for Christian leadership.

I have always regarded students as my chief teachers. I have learned from them far more than I have taught. My philosophy of education is that I teach students, not subjects. Oh, yes, I use certain subjects or disciplines to teach them, but I must never forget where my challenge lies. Students are the ones who have raised the questions I have tried to answer in this book. They have helped me to see the real issues at stake in the world and in the church today. They have kept me in touch with reality, sometimes when they have not listened as well as when they have.

I am indebted to many persons for what you will find here. At the head of the list are ordinary saints who have left their prints all over my life—especially Fleta and Osse Marsh, my aunt and uncle, who lived what they believed; Bertha Brown, my teacher in a one-room country school in the Missouri Ozarks, who gave me an example of faithfulness beyond compare; G. C. Busch, the owner of the country store five miles from our farm, who kept my family alive during the depression; but also a row of others. Next, some extraordinary saints who helped me see a way to get my head and my heart together as I climbed some high mountains in a most earnest quest to know God—Huston Smith, my professor at Washington University in St. Louis, whose world-embracing faith carried me beyond a crisis of faith at age nineteen; Thomas Merton, monk at

Gethsemani in Kentucky, who awakened me to the necessity of a life of prayer in a world of action; Douglas Steere, an extraordinary Friend and friend, who reached out to buoy me up and to confirm what is deepest in me; S. L. Greenslade, my guide in the study of early Christian history at Oxford, who demonstrated in his own life that one can be both saint and scholar. My fellow members of the Ecumenical Institute of Spirituality founded by Douglas Steere and Godfrey Diekmann, O.S.B., during the Second Vatican Council, have inspired and informed all of my contributions in this area for the last quarter century. I will never be able adequately to put into words my inexpressible thanks to God that I have lived and taught in the incredible era opened by the pontificate of John XXIII and the Second Vatican Council. Thanks be to God for this gift that defies description!

For the invitation to write *Spiritual Preparation for Christian Leadership* I must thank The Upper Room and George Donigian, my editor. Baptist Theological Seminary at Richmond has assisted immensely in arranging a schedule that would permit me blocks of time to write. The outstanding William Smith Morton Library of Union Theological Seminary in Richmond has given me easy access to materials that I needed beyond my personal files and library. First Baptist Church, Greenville, South Carolina, permitted me to write three chapters of this book while I served as Spiritual Director in Residence, in January and February 1998, and showed me in the vital interest they took in lectures on the subject of spirituality how important spiritual preparation is for Christian leadership. Stephanie Ford, a former student, now a graduate student in spirituality at Catholic University of America, and Sonja Matthews, a current student, have read and offered suggestions about the manuscript.

E. Glenn Hinson
May 21, 1998

Chapter 1

IS SPIRITUAL FORMATION NEEDED?

In 1960 shortly after I took my first group of church history students at the Southern Baptist Theological Seminary in Louisville to visit the Abbey of Gethsemani, Thomas Merton mailed me about ten or twelve manuals he used to teach novices and an autographed copy of *Spiritual Direction and Meditation*. I thumbed through the manuals and read *Spiritual Direction and Meditation* without perceiving in the slightest way that the books might have some relevance to what I or my colleagues at Southern Seminary were doing in preparing Christian leaders. Spiritual formation and direction sounded alien and authoritarian to the ears of a person of Free Church background and persuasion, where the voluntary principle stands at the center. Notwithstanding how much I liked Thomas Merton himself and the peacefulness I found in his monastery, what he said about spiritual direction sailed right over my head without touching a single hair.

A few years later, the Association of Theological Schools in the United States and Canada, aided by grants from the Lilly Foundation, sponsored Charles F. Whiston, Professor of Moral Theology at the Church Divinity School of the Pacific, in conducting schools of prayer among Protestant seminarians. In those "secular sixties" some students thought Professor Whiston's efforts quite alien to where they lived. After he had lectured about prayer for about an hour in a school conducted at Earlham College in Richmond, Indiana, one student blurted out, "I don't know why we waste our time talking about prayer. When I kiss my wife, that's a prayer. When I take out the garbage, that's a prayer." The "secular sixties" did not smile on the separating of sacred and secular realms.

As ecumenical trends prompted Protestants and Catholics to seek opportunities for sharing, TEAM-A (the Theological Education Association of Mid-America) sponsored one meeting on spirituality. Father Camillus Ellspermann, O.S.B., of St. Meinrad School of Theology in Indiana presented a paper recounting the Benedictine approach to formation for the priesthood. As one of the respondents, I remember how strong was my note of caution—almost fear—lest Protestants give up their birthright to adopt means and methods that seemed to threaten the central tenets of the Reformation. In the eighties still, at a conference conducted by Tilden Edwards, founder of Shalem in Washington, D.C., I sounded the concern I have not abandoned that whatever we adopt in the way of formation, it must square with the essence of our tradition, namely, the voluntary principle in religion.

Today I teach a course at Baptist Theological Seminary at Richmond entitled "Ministers as Spiritual Guides" in which students read Merton's *Spiritual Direction and Meditation* with comprehension and interest. Not only so, I am envisioning the gradual development of a program for spiritual formation of Christian leaders similar to what you would find in Roman Catholic seminaries, though perhaps not quite as heavy, where the spiritual formation of the person would play a leading role in the overall preparation for ministry. At the suggestion of alumni

I am projecting a half-credit (two-hour-a-week) requirement in spirituality each semester that would begin with an introduction to spirituality (how to pray, journaling, spirituality and personality, spirituality and sexuality, balance in the spiritual life) and then proceed with the history of spirituality, the theology of religious experience, the psychology of spirituality, the classics of Christian devotion, and end with ministers as spiritual guides. All of these classes would seek to integrate theory and practice, learning by doing. Although I cannot yet envision how a Protestant seminary such as ours might also require each student to have an individual spiritual guide throughout the years in seminary, given the fact that there are not many experienced guides around, some Protestant seminaries are able to offer group guidance, and some students can obtain one-on-one guidance.

Protestants have moved cautiously and reluctantly in this direction over the span of thirty or forty years. When I entered Southern Seminary as a B.D. (now M.Div.) student in 1954, the old Body of Divinity still held sway with practical studies—pastoral care, church administration, religious education, church music—trying to creep in and gain credibility. Personal piety of ministers may have gotten some boost through corporate worship, exhortations of professors or administrators, and felt needs of students themselves, but fears of pseudospirituality and sanctimonious shibboleths dampened openness to spiritual growth and development. Better a sophisticated secularity than false piety or, worse still, works righteousness. How does one explain the leap from caution, indifference, and even hostility toward spiritual formation to faltering steps to make it an important part of training of Christian leaders?

Changing Ecumenical Climate

One obvious reason for this gigantic shift in Protestant attitudes toward spiritual formation is the massive shift in Protestant and Catholic attitudes toward each other since Pope John XXIII (1958–63) launched his "New Pentecost." Prior to Pope John and the Second Vatican Council (1962–65), Catholic seminaries charted one course, Protestant seminaries another. According to a study done by Walter D. Wagoner under sponsorship of the Fund for Theological Education in the early sixties, Catholic seminaries placed spiritual formation at the center of the curriculum. They sought to be "that place, those years, wherein the seminarians are helped to devotional and spiritual maturity." On the average, Catholic seminarians spent five times as much time in spiritual exercises as their Protestant counterparts.[1] Protestant seminaries focused on educating ministers in the traditional Body of Divinity and skills for ministry and offered little that would qualify as spiritual formation. Wagoner quoted one prominent student leader at Union Theological Seminary in New York:

> Union is very much like the world, apart from relative unity of commitment to some form of ministry of Jesus Christ. The chapel is not central to most of us, regardless of how much we may talk about the necessity of some sort of authentic worship. Darn few students partake in any self-styled personal religious discipline. Action is more prominent than prayer; Harvey Cox is more closely studied than St. Paul. Retreats are relatively infrequent as opposed to the protests of ad hoc social and political action groups.

---

[1] Walter D. Wagoner, *The Seminary, Protestant and Catholic* (New York: Sheed and Ward, 1966), 24-25.

Union students are on the go, trying to juggle an incredible number of outside or extra-curricular commitments together with a respectable amount of required academic assignments. To this extent, Union is very much like the world outside.[2]

The Second Vatican Council wrought a startling change in Roman Catholic perspectives and in ecumenical relations. After centuries of living in relative isolation and hurling thunderbolts from secure bunkers, Catholics and Protestants now sought out one another to get to know one another and to exchange ideas and to seek solutions to common problems. The healthiest and most lasting gain from these exchanges for Protestants has been in the area of spirituality and spiritual formation. Concepts of Christian leadership will continue to distinguish Catholics and Protestants, but they are converging in their concern for spiritual formation of leaders.

The Fourth Awakening

Accompanying and augmenting this ecumenical tide has been what historians call an "awakening," the fourth such in American history.[3] The first was the Great Awakening, which lasted from about 1720 until 1760; followed by the Frontier Revival, sometimes called the Second Great Awakening, which flared up between 1790 and 1820; and the Social Gospel movement of the late nineteenth and early twentieth centuries.

---

[2] Ibid., 31.

[3] See on this William G. McGlothlin, *Revivals, Awakenings, and Reform* (Chicago: University of Chicago Press, 1978), 141ff.

Awakenings usually go through three stages. The current awakening sprang out of the confusion, disorder, and despair connected with the turbulent years of the Vietnam War era— antiwar protests, violence in the cities, the civil rights movement, and other happenings. There followed in the seventies and eighties a deepened religious search directed not only toward finding deeper insight in the Judeo-Christian tradition but toward the wisdom of Oriental religions— Buddhism, Hinduism, Taoism, and many others. In the nineties has emerged the change of consciousness that awakenings effect—global awareness and cries for freedom and sharing of the world's resources.

Behind this change of consciousness lies a massive revolution in technology even greater than Gutenberg's invention of movable type in 1456 on the eve of the Reformation of the sixteenth century. Because of advances in communication—satellites, televisions, computers, the World Wide Web—we can no longer conduct our lives as citizens of one country, certainly not of one small province of a country, oblivious to the needs of the rest of the world. We must live as *world* citizens, eyewitnesses and participants in what is happening everywhere. The war in the Persian Gulf was the first that Americans actually witnessed live! We saw with our own eyes the explosions of "smart bombs" and the incineration of people in a marketplace. We've also seen firsthand the massacre of innocents in Rwanda, the starving of masses in Ethiopia, and the fall of the Berlin Wall.

Baby Boomers and Gen Xers

The chief representatives of this postmodern culture are the baby boomers and Gen Xers or baby busters. Boomers are persons born between 1946 and 1964, Gen Xers those born between 1965 and 1977.

According to sociologist Wade Clark Roof, baby boomers altered the religious landscape of the United States in the 1990s.[4] Although by no means monolithic, divided along lines of age, education, economic class, gender, lifestyle, and even chronologically, they display enough commonalities to merit the designation of "a generation of seekers." (1) They emphasize the inner versus the outer world. (2) They seek to recover the spiritual, convinced that inner experience is the wellspring of authentic religious life. (3) They have about the same level of belief in God as others but are less dogmatic and oppose stifling orthodoxy. (4) They distinguish sharply between the "religious" and the "spiritual"—"religious" having an institutional connotation, "spiritual" a more personal one. (5) Some are highly active seekers who are deeply involved in their own quest and prefer mystical religion because it is more open, personal, and adaptable. Churches that attract boomers are more open and make room for spiritual growth. "Boomers are hungry to find ways to commit themselves," Roof concluded, "if they can find personal enhancement, or extension of their own selves, in whatever they do or in however they give of themselves."[5] The church of the future is not the megachurch but the metachurch, one with traditional structures within which there is room for small groups that can respond to the quest of boomers.

The members of Generation X, which some have labeled the "first post-Christian generation," seem to follow in the train of their parents except for an added dash of cynicism. Pollster George Barna referred to baby busters as "More than

---

[4] Wade Clark Roof, *A Generation of Seekers* (San Francisco: Harper/Collins, 1992), 1.

[5] Ibid., 247.

any prior generation, they feel estranged from God, separated from each other, lacking meaning in life, void of roots and a societal connection. In short, they feel alienated from life."[6] Many were reared in dysfunctional families, educated in deteriorating schools, and face poorer economic prospects than their parents. They are the first generation to grow up in the midst of the postmodern, anti-Enlightenment culture. Whereas modernism counted on certain, objective, good, and attainable knowledge, postmodernism operates on the primary assumption that truth is attainable not only by intellect but also by emotion and intuition.[7] Each individual and the community to which he or she belongs can define truth, so the accent rests on community.

A Baby Buster Consultation sponsored by InterVarsity Christian Fellowship and Leighton Ford Ministries in 1993 discerned five major characteristics in baby buster spirituality: authenticity, community, lack of dogmatism, focus on the arts, and diversity. (1) Gen Xers are not content with simplistic answers to life's complex questions. They know life is hard, and they want honesty in facing it. (2) Like baby boomers, they crave community. They are "homesick" for the home they never knew. They focus on relationships rather than achievement. (3) Barna reported, "To the typical Buster, there is no such thing as absolute truth."[8] Most look askance at dogmatism, whether regarding scriptures, belief in God, church doctrine, or the absoluteness of Christianity. (4) Busters see in the arts, especially music, a way to get in touch with God. The arts provide an emotional experience of God and a prime means of

---

[6] George Barna, *Baby Busters: The Disillusioned Generation* (Chicago: Northfield Publishing, 1994), 72.

[7] Stanley Grenz, *A Primer on Postmodernism* (Grand Rapids: Wm. B. Eerdmans, 1996).

[8] Barna, *Baby Busters*, 69.

worship. (5) Finally, they seek authenticity in society and church fractured by racial and other divisions. Once again, like baby boomers, they accept and affirm diversity.[9]

A Vocation with High Expectations

Christian ministry has always been a daunting vocation in which who you are matters more than what you know or what skills you may have. You can see in the Pastoral Epistles why that is so in the exhortation to Timothy to "set the believers an example in speech and conduct, in love, in faith, in purity" (1 Tim. 4:12). Applied to the present day, in an age of misspeak, gross speak, down speak, and outright lying, be a model in what you say. Speak the truth in love (Eph. 4:15). "Let your word be 'Yes, Yes' or 'No, No'" (Matt. 5:37). Let your word be your bond. In an age when politicians and preachers establish new records in ethical sleaze, be above reproach, honorable in all your dealings. In an age of gross abuse and wanton violence, make love your aim. "Love is patient; love is kind; love is not envious or boastful or arrogant or rude. It does not insist on its own way; it is not irritable or resentful; it does not rejoice in wrongdoing, but rejoices in the truth" (1 Cor. 13:4-6). In an age when covenants are broken almost as quickly as they are made, stand by your commitments. Do not be blown about by every wind. Be steadfast. In an age of sexual exhibitionism, exploitation, pruriency, and license, exemplify faithfulness in this most intimate of all human relationships.

---

[9] Reported by Andres Tapia, "Reaching the First Post-Christian Generation," *Christianity Today*, September 12, 1994, 23-28. See also Jim Belcher, "It's the Gospel, Stupid: Generation X and Religion," *Regeneration Quarterly*, spring 1995, 23-26.

Expectations for Christian ministry have not diminished. If anything, personal expectations have become more demanding than ever. *A Readiness for Ministry* survey sponsored by the Association of Theological Schools in the United States and Canada confirmed the priority of the personal in evaluating ministers. Nearly all of the nine positive and all three negative criteria focused primarily on personal factors. Positive criteria were (1) "service without regard for acclaim"; (2) personal integrity, that is, ability "to honor commitments by carrying out promises despite all pressures to compromise"; (3) belief in the gospel that "manifests itself in generosity, and in general, a Christian example that people in the community can respect"; (4) displaying "competence and responsibility by completing tasks, by being able to handle differences of opinions" and sensing "the need to continue to grow in pastoral skills"; (5) leadership in "building a strong sense of community within a congregation"; (6) counseling "as one who reaches out to persons under stress with a perception, sensitivity, and warmth that is freeing and supportive"; (7) willingness to "sharpen an already keen intelligence through continual theological study and careful attention to clarity of thought and expression"; (8) ability "to handle stressful situations by remaining calm under pressure while continuing to affirm persons"; and (9) ability "to acknowledge limitations and mistakes and recognize the need for continued growth and learning."[10] The factors that drew severe criticism were (1) being self-serving, "a minister who avoids intimacy and repels people with a critical, demeaning, and insensitive attitude"; (2) engaging in "illicit sexual relationships and other self-indulgent actions that irritate, shock, or offend"; and (3) displaying

---

[10] David S. Schuler, Milo L. Brekke, and Merton P. Strommen, *Readiness for Ministry, vol. 1--Criteria* (Vandalia, Ohio: Association of Theological Schools in the United States and Canada, 1975), 6-7.

"emotional immaturity and actions that demonstrate immaturity, insecurity, and insensitivity when buffeted by the demands and pressures of the profession."[11]

A Stressful Vocation

Given such high expectations, no one should be surprised to learn that Christian leadership can be filled with stress. Roy Oswald has put his finger on stress experienced by pastors:

> Pastors are in a people-related profession in which our value to others is our ability to get down in the trenches with them when the bombs are dropping all around. In addition to being there for people through all the joys and traumas of their lives, we are expected somehow, by magic, to keep everybody happy and make our congregations grow. All of this in a post-Christian/Jewish culture that no longer holds in high esteem men and women of the cloth. If we are not stressed to a greater or lesser degree, we aren't in touch with reality.[12]

A high percentage of those who undertake leadership roles in the church burn out, are forced out or fired, or simply resign themselves to a halfhearted job.

Burnout, spiritual exhaustion, in ministry has received much attention since the eighties when its frequency captured the attention of psychologists. The more dedicated you are, the more likely you are to consume all of the energy you have, often

---

[11] Ibid., 7-8.

[12] Roy M. Oswald, *Clergy Self-Care: Finding a Balance for Effective Ministry* (New York: Alban Institute, 1991), 26.

pressing on when you have run out of fuel. It is very easy in ministry to fall into what Carmen Renee Berry and Mark Lloyd Taylor call "the Messiah Trap" in which you convince yourself of two lies: "If I don't do it, it won't get done" and "Everyone else's needs take priority over mine."[13] Churches, which should help to spring people from the Messiah Trap, all too often set it, particularly for ministers.

The number of ministers forced to resign or fired by churches has reached alarming proportions in recent years. Many of the separations take place after years of faithful service when ministers have great difficulty relocating. Factors behind the firing of ministers are too complex to be discussed here. Some originate in the corporation motif wherein ministers are considered hired hands who can be fired if they don't "do the job." Others stem from personal tensions between ministers and their people. Others arise out of denominational dynamics, for example, a conservative group asserting itself with encouragement of others in the denomination to force out a more liberal minister. Still others spring up out of local issues in the community that spill over into the churches. Whatever the causes, the terminations inflict terrible pain and suffering. Some denominations have structures that may cushion these blows, but those with congregational polity do not, and congregations often take little thought about a hard landing.

Others manage to survive in ministry by accommodating themselves to difficult situations. Instead of offering leadership, they "go along to get along." They avoid challenging and prophetic thoughts and actions. They compromise convictions in order to keep their positions.

---

13 Carmen Renee Berry and Mark Lloyd Taylor, *Loving Yourself as Your Neighbor: A Recovery Guide for Christians Escaping Burnout and Codependency* (San Francisco: Harper & Row, 1990), 12.

Whither This Book?

This book is being written in the conviction that spirituality can help to meet the urgent needs of Christian churches and ministers. The Apostle Paul was right: "Such is the confidence that we have through Christ toward God. Not that we are competent of ourselves to claim anything as coming from us; our competence is from God, who has made us competent to be ministers of a new covenant" (2 Cor. 3:4-6).

Chapter 2 will review the history of spiritual formation for Christian leadership. Chapter 3 will focus on the main issue in spiritual preparation—a relationship with God. Subsequent chapters will consider ways for you to hold yourself accountable through journal keeping (4); making the best use of your time (5); maintaining balance of experiential, intellectual, social, and institutional dimensions (6); and fostering a healthy relationship between sexuality and spirituality (7). Three chapters will suggest ways to sustain the spiritual life through spiritual reading, listening, and seeing (8); solitude and silence (9); and spiritual friendship (10). A concluding chapter will reflect on the broader issue of what the world and the church need most (11). An appendix will offer some guidance concerning personality and spirituality.

Chapter 2

SPIRITUAL FORMATION OF CHRISTIAN LEADERS IN HISTORY

The spiritual formation of Christian leaders has been a matter of prime importance throughout the history of Christianity, but it has not always received the kind of conscious consideration it is getting today. There has been enough reflection at critical periods, however, to mark out the history into several decisive epochs. The first phase, covering roughly the first three centuries, was a period in which spiritual formation took place on the job in a risky occupation. In the next phase, from the fourth century to the end of the Middle Ages, monasticism supplied the chief model. Thereafter, in the third phase, as determined by the Council of Trent (1545–63), Catholics reaffirmed the medieval model. Protestants, attempting to return to earliest Christian practices and fearful of lapsing into approaches that would threaten the priesthood of believers, regarded spiritual formation with considerable suspicion. The problems generated by a lapse of conscious attention to this aspect of the training of ministers, consequently, evoked the rethinking of spirituality in German Pietism and in the development of Protestant seminaries. Yet the emphasis of

Pietism on spiritual formation of Christian leaders had modest effect on Protestantism as a whole. Protestant leaders, therefore, have found themselves poorly equipped to meet overwhelming demands placed upon them in a century of ever-increasing deadliness in warfare, incredible advances in science and technology, alienation and polarization, and a confusing array of other things.

Out of experiences in concentration camps during the Second World War, Protestants and Catholics began to rediscover and learn from one another. In regard to spiritual preparation for Christian leadership, they have drunk anew at some of the same rich streams that have nourished the faithful through the centuries. The churches are discovering anew that to be effective in ministry to other persons, they have to be well formed as *persons*. On the basis of this premise, your spiritual training as a Christian leader cannot be detached from the rest of your preparation. Spiritual formation has to do not with the shaping of a compartment of your life but with the rounding out of the personality, the whole self, in Jesus Christ.

On-the-Job Training in an Age of Martyrs

In the first three centuries the training of Christian leaders occurred on the job. Selection was governed usually by evidences of spirituality during the catechumenate. In this age of martyrs the catechumenate had to prepare converts literally to die for their faith.[1] Any who assumed leadership roles were particularly vulnerable, especially from the Decian persecution (250–51) on. Leaders had to sustain a high level of commitment through corporate worship, prayer, Bible reading, and other

---

[1] On the development of the three-year catechumenate see E. Glenn Hinson, *The Evangelization of the Roman Empire* (Macon, Ga.: Mercer University Press, 1981), 73-87.

means, thus setting an example for others. The older leaders usually gave guidance to the younger.

This model possibly harked back to Jesus' calling and training of disciples. T. W. Manson argues that, whereas Jesus' teaching was directed at first to a larger audience, after Caesarea-Philippi Jesus directed that teaching to an inner circle of disciples.[2] Whether or not Manson's thesis is right, many passages in the Gospels reflect Jesus' schooling of his close followers. What training they received, they obtained in the company of Jesus. Following Jesus was their "seminary."

In the main the disciples' formation must have come from the total impact of the varied situations that they confronted with the master. They learned the significance of prayer or other acts of symbolic devotion, therefore, from seeing them in the life of Jesus, an observant Jew with a strong divine consciousness. If we may trust the impression left by the Synoptic Gospels, Jesus implanted in their minds the necessity of a profound God-awareness in all of life that was to be sharpened by prayer and other acts of worship.

The next several generations of Christian leaders obtained their spiritual formation in a similar manner. The specific examples that come to our attention next were missionaries. Since Paul offers the most detailed evidence, let his pattern illuminate our discussion. Paul employed a parental pattern for those who assisted him in the Gentile mission. He mentored his associates like a mature parent. He cared deeply about each of them and watched over their growth in faith and life. Silvanus or Silas, Timothy, and Titus were his "sons" in the faith. Timothy, whose rather insecure personality made him more dependent than others, got special care. On the critical Corinthian mission Paul built him up as "my beloved and faithful child in the Lord, who shall remind you of my ways in

---

[2] T. W. Manson, *The Teaching of Jesus* (Cambridge: Cambridge University Press, 1955), 12ff.

Christ" (1 Cor. 4:17). Similarly, he expressed a hope that he could send Timothy, his *alter ego*, to Philippi to remind them of his situation, for "I have no one like him" (Phil. 2:20). Silas, Timothy, and Titus should imitate his example even as Paul imitated Christ's.

The Pastoral Epistles, thought by many to be the work of an admirer of Paul, also depict an intimate father-son relationship between Paul and Timothy. Timothy was Paul's heir apparent in the Ephesian mission, and the Apostle sought to give the paternal advice by which the younger man could carry on there. His instructions combined practical and personal counsel. Intermingled with directions regarding community organization were commands concerning "spiritual training" of the "person of God" (cf. 1 Tim. 4:7-10; 6:11-16) according to Paul's model. Second Timothy 3:10-11 is especially illuminating: "Now you have observed my teaching, my conduct, my aim in life, my faith, my patience, my love, my steadfastness, my persecutions and suffering the things that happened to me in Antioch, Iconium, and Lystra. What persecutions I endured!" Timothy had been schooled on the job with Paul.

As early Christianity's situation became more settled in having established communities with a resident clergy, the responsibility for the training of ministers fell upon the shoulders of the clergy themselves, especially the bishop. No formal schools were designed specifically for the training of the clergy. Some training, it is true, could and did occur in philosophical or evangelistic schools, such as that at Alexandria developed by Pantaenus during the second century, that at Rome founded by Justin Martyr around 150 C.E., or that at Caesarea Maritima established by Origen when he moved there from Alexandria in 232. Several presbyters and bishops—for instance, Demetrius in Alexandria and Gregory of Neocaesarea, the Miracle Worker, in Caesarea—had some of their basic formation in these. Gregory paid tribute to Origen not simply as an apologist and teacher but for his profound personal impact.[3] As his approach to scriptures makes quite clear, Origen focused, above all, on spiritual formation. In the first two or three centuries it is quite possible that other schools trained a number of missionaries and resident clergy,[4] but the schools were not primarily for the clergy.

Whatever role the "schools" might have played in the spiritual formation of Christian leaders, the center of this activity soon came to rest in the bishop as the chief shepherd of the Christian flock in a city or province. The letters of Cyprian, the bishop of Carthage, addressed to his presbyters and deacons while hiding during the Decian persecution, make transparent the kind of training that went on all the time. Cyprian, like Paul, offered a fatherly example as well as direct counsel or instruction. Furthermore, his clergy formed a kind of community of faith in which such formation would occur regularly. In his earlier years as a bishop, Cyprian professed to give careful heed to the opinions of both the clergy and his people. He refused, for example, to render a judgment on a sensitive matter brought to his attention by several presbyters, "since from the first commencement of my episcopacy, I made up my mind to do nothing on my own private opinion, without your [the clergy's] advice and without the consent of the people."[5]

Bishops such as Cyprian placed the highest priority on spiritual exercises that could equip the clergy for their risky roles. Persecution reinforced this conviction, for the great bishop witnessed many of his clergy as well as the laity apostatize in the face of torture. One of his letters pleaded urgently with his

---

[3] Gregory Thaumaturgus *Panegyric on Origen.*

[4] One example is a school at Antioch that Krister Stendahl, *The School of St. Matthew and Its Use of the Old Testament* (Lund: C. W. K. Gleerup, 1954), thinks was formed to train such persons and produced the Gospel according to Matthew for that purpose.

[5] Cyprian *Epistle.* 5.4; The Ante-Nicene Fathers, V:283.

clergy to "pray and groan with continual petitions" after the example of Jesus and Paul.[6]

A Monastic Model

The rapid expansion of Christian leadership in response to a massive influx of new members during a long era of peace in the late third century (ca. 260–303 C.E.) and then after the conversion of Constantine in 312 overtaxed this rather informal system of formation. From the early fourth century on, councils of bishops gave extensive consideration to qualifications and rules of conduct for clergy. These offered some guidance but, judging by their content, hardly more than guidance of an elementary nature in spiritual formation.

The model for spiritual formation of the clergy that soon dominated came from monasticism, which began to develop as Christian discipline declined with the cessation of persecution and the mushrooming of church membership. The monastic influence may be seen in the fourth-century disciplinary canons that, in the West but not in the East, at first urged and thereafter sought to enforce clerical celibacy. Cenobite or communal monasticism, which bishops such as Basil of Caesarea espoused, offered a model that the clergy could and did adopt for their training.

This critical development took place in the West, where the Germanic invasions and other historical factors exaggerated a widespread pessimism and made flight from the "world" a highly attractive option for masses of people. Ambrose of Milan, among other bishops, inculcated the monastic ideal among his clergy. However, Augustine opened the way for it to become the standard of spirituality for many centuries. His patterning of his

---

[6] Cyprian *Ep*. 7.5; ANF, V:286.

clerical community at Hippo on a monastic model assured that the formation of the clergy would be like the formation of monks and, indeed, that monasticism would supply thereafter a large portion of Christian leadership. The immense contribution of monks and monasteries to the spread of Christianity in the Middle Ages reinforced further the prominence of their role in all medieval life.

Augustine became a presbyter during a period of crisis in North African Christianity. The threat of Manichaeism and the Donatist schism merely added to the crisis of spiritual indifference and moral decay. An important part of the practical response to this situation rested in a committed, well-trained clergy. The obvious model for this lay at hand in monasticism. Thus, when Augustine accepted ordination, according to his biographer Possidius, he soon founded a monastery within the church of Hippo and "began to live there among the servants of God according to the rule and custom established by the holy Apostles."[7] The chief regulation imposed community of goods. The exemplary lives of Augustine and his clergy, Possidius claims, wielded enough influence in Hippo to attract the attention of other churches. The latter began to turn to this community for bishops and presbyters, who carried with them the monastic idea.

During the Middle Ages, the formation of the clergy occurred, therefore, in either of two contexts—monastic or episcopal schools. Monastic schools aimed principally at spiritual formation and tended even to undervalue or criticize liberal culture. The fact that monks did more than any other medieval group to conserve the foundations of learning does not contradict this fact, for most of what they conserved, even of classical learning, had to do with its values for piety. Accordingly, when Charlemagne sought to broaden the base of

---

[7] Possidius *Life of Augustine* 5, translated by Mary Magdalene Muller, O.S.F., and Roy J. DeFerrari (New York: Fathers of the Church, Inc., 1952), 78.

education within the Frankish kingdom, he had to insist that the monastic schools, which he used for his program, teach more than the Bible and monastic prayer routines. The monastic regimen according to the Rule of Benedict, which dominated medieval monasticism, consisted in the main of the *Opus Dei*, chanting of the Psalms at the established times; the *lectio divina*, meditation on scriptures and other writings; and manual labor.

Training in episcopal schools did not differ notably from that in monastic schools once the monastic model came to prevail. It was really through the instrumentality of outstanding monks, many of whom became leading clergy, that education became more academic. The British monk Alcuin, for example, was the genius behind Charlemagne's revival of learning. Similarly, the universities originated and began to take prominent places through the efforts of outstanding monks such as Anselm of Canterbury (ca. 1033–1109), Anselm of Laon (d. 1117), William of Champeaux (ca. 1070–1121), Peter Abelard (1079–1142), John of Salisbury (ca. 1115–80), and many others. Most of them received their education in monastic schools such as the famous one located in the Abbey of Bec, France, whose first two abbots were Lanfranc and Anselm, or cathedral schools such as that located in Paris.

The universities, although growing out of monastic and cathedral schools, gradually exerted an educational pull away from contemplative piety and toward a more or less rigorous academic training. Although only a limited number of the clergy received this kind of instruction, scholasticism tended to supplant monasticism as the model in education. The late Middle Ages, like many other periods of history, saw the pendulum swing from one end of the arc to the other as the brighter clergy acquired an understanding of religion that stood far above the level of comprehension of the virtually illiterate masses, even above that of many clergy. Added to the plethora of other problems in the church during the eleventh through thirteenth centuries, this gap helped to prepare the conditions for a major revolution in piety and in the formation of the clergy.

Catholic Continuance of the Medieval Pattern

At the Council of Trent the Spanish model of reform devised by Cardinal Ximenes, archbishop of Toledo and confessor of Queen Isabella, won out over the Italian model. Ximenes emphasized revival of scholastic theology through establishment of new universities, moral renewal of the clergy, and revitalization of commitment through the Inquisition. Baroque art and architecture used overstatement to underline the importance of loyalty to the church. It called attention to the altar, the sacraments, and ultimately the church as the sure director of souls. The chief agents through whom the church countered the impact of the Protestant Reformation, however, were members of the Society of Jesus founded by Ignatius Loyola. In the post-Reformation era Loyola's *Spiritual Exercises*, devised during a period of agonized religious search in 1521–22, established the main lines for spiritual formation.

The *Spiritual Exercises* laid out a rigorous plan for forming devout and disciplined followers of Jesus. It combined spiritual direction and careful self-examination to root out faults with meditation on the life of Jesus and various forms of prayer. Its rigors, however, necessitated adaptation to be of use to laypersons. Francis de Sales crafted a gentler approach more amenable to laypersons in his *Introduction to the Devout Life* (1621). Jesuit zeal on the church's behalf in a time of rising nationalism also evoked a lot of negative reaction that led briefly to the disbanding of the order from 1773 to 1814. Nevertheless, the Ignatian method, applied in varying ways, continued to exert massive influence in the forming of Catholic leadership throughout the post-Reformation period.

Search for a Protestant Model

Because the Protestant Reformers closed the monasteries, they needed a new model for education of Protestant leaders. In theory they opted for the perspective of the devotio moderna, which had been developing in conjunction with the revival of classical learning during the fourteenth and fifteenth centuries. The *devotio moderna* stressed the practice of Christianity instead of salvation through the sacraments and the offices of the church.

Desiderius Erasmus, the most widely acknowledged representative of humanism during the early sixteenth century, set the model that most markedly influenced the shape of Protestant clerical formation. Like other humanists, Erasmus conceived of religion as a doctrine of life rather than a mysterious redemption. Personally, he wedded the piety of the German and Dutch mystics (exemplified in the *Imitation of Christ*) with classical humanism. He did not abandon the sacraments and the traditions of the church, but neither did he feel slavishly bound to them. Erasmus thought ecclesiastical ceremonies permissible for the "simple," the "weak," or "infant" Christians, but he insisted that "God is not pleased by anything but the invisible state of righteousness."[8] Erasmus placed his premium upon the scriptures. He once told a friend who wanted him to return to the monastery that he was "determined to live

---

[8] Erasmus *Enchiridion XIV*, trans. Raymond Himelick (Bloomington, Ind.: Indiana University Press, 1963), 176.

and die in the study of Sacred Scriptures."[9] He envisioned his role as that of a sixteenth-century Jerome. For Erasmus, Christ is the teacher. He is known from the scriptures. Therefore, it is especially by education in the scriptures that one will be led to practice one's religion. Undoubtedly, Erasmus's greatest contribution to sixteenth-century Christianity was his endeavor to place the scriptures at the disposal of the common person. By having access to the scriptures, he was convinced, common persons will live as they ought. In line with this conviction Erasmus derided the pillars of clerical education in the Middle Ages—monasticism and scholasticism. Perhaps because of unhappy experiences he had had while attached to the Order of White Canons, he could see no special merit in monastic vows and thought Christians could fulfill their vocation as well or better in the world than in a monastery. Likewise, he was critical of teachers in the universities. He would not abolish their endeavors, but he could see in them little that produced edification in matters of importance.[10]

This kind of thinking, widely diffused in the early sixteenth century, influenced Protestant clerical education. Subsequently, until the nineteenth century, Protestant clergy obtained their training in universities where education was shaped by the Erasmian model. At Wittenberg, for example, Luther and Melanchthon, his Erasmian associate, saw that both Hebrew and Greek culture became a part of the required studies. Lewis Spitz has concluded, "If Luther saw the threat of an Erasmian culture-religion and spotted the dangerous symptoms even in the naive fusion of culture and religion in the Brethren of the Common Life, he nevertheless appreciated the great value

---

[9] Erasmus *Epistle to Servatius Roger*, July 8, 1514, in Erasmus and His Age, ed. Hans J. Hillerbrand (New York: Harper & Row, 1970), 73.
[10] See his *Epistle to Paul Volz*, August 18, 1518.

of culture as culture, and of culture put into the service of the church."[11]

The element of clerical training that Luther and the other Protestant Reformers seem to have let slip or perhaps deliberately left to chance was precisely spiritual formation. Once a reader and admirer of devotional classics such as *The German Theology*, which he published twice (in 1518 and 1523), and *The Imitation of Christ*, Luther now insisted upon focusing the entire spiritual formation of the Christian upon one book, the Bible. He condemned with extreme harshness the monastic exercises that he had once used to cultivate his own piety as devilish means of works salvation. Similarly, he condemned observance of the church's fasts, prayers, pilgrimages, masses, vigils, charitable endowments, and other devotional media. It was a partial contradiction, then, when Luther himself continued to pursue a rigorous pattern of devotion focused upon reading the Psalms, using the Lord's Prayer as a devotional stimulus, and treating the Ten Commandments as a guide to doctrine, a hymnbook, a confessional book, and a prayer book.[12]

Not long after the Protestant movement had gotten under way, Luther and other Reformers came to recognize the liabilities of unstructured piety. Common persons of the Middle Ages had learned to rely on prayer books to help them with their devotion. When they heard the Protestant Reformers fulminate against their use, they turned to the Reformers themselves for substitutes. To supply such a demand, Luther, for example, produced his *Seven Penitential Psalms with a German Translation* (1517), circulated several sermons, composed a *Short Form of the Ten Commandments, the Creed, and the Lord's*

---

[11] Lewis W. Spitz, *The Religious Renaissance of the German Humanists* (Cambridge, Mass.: Harvard University Press, 1963), 246.
[12] See his letter to Peter Beskendorf, composed in early 1535, *Library of Christian Classics*, XVIII:124-30.

Prayer (1520), and compiled or wrote his *Personal Prayer Book* (1522). He also penned a large number of letters to both laypersons and clergy.[13]

Exactly how much of this sort of spiritual counsel carried over into the training of ministers in Protestantism is debatable. Spiritual formation was left largely in the hands of individual faculty members in the universities, where the clergy received their principal training. As long as the faculty assumed a measure of responsibility for this, as Luther and other Protestant leaders did, no serious failings occurred. When Protestantism leaped into its own brand of scholasticism in which academic concerns preempted concern for spiritual formation, however, the education of the clergy suffered accordingly.

The Seminary Model

The next phase in spiritual formation of Protestant leaders became an attempt to recover some elements lost when the Reformers abandoned the monastic model in favor of a more this-worldly and less spiritually formative way of training ministers. In some respects this process has continued from the seventeenth century on, but it is well illustrated in the proposals of the father of German Pietism, Philip Jacob Spener (1635–1705), and in the establishment of Protestant theological schools or seminaries.

Spener thought the revitalization of Lutheran churches would depend on Bible study and cultivation of the inner life in small cell groups (*collegia pietatis*), more extensive lay involvement in the life of the churches, less rhetorical and more

---

13 See *Luther's Works*, vol. 43, ed. Gustav K. Wiencke (Philadelphia: Fortress Press, 1968).

practical preaching, more respectful treatment of unbelievers, and radical reshaping of the training of ministers.

Among the proposals that he made for the rescue of the churches from the deadening grip of "pharisaic orthodoxy," Spener gave by far the most precise attention to the improvement of ministerial education at the point of their spiritual formation. Spener said that he was keenly aware of the crucial role played by the clergy in the renewal of the churches. This made their training in piety all the more crucial. Like others, Spener was scandalized that the preparatory schools and the universities tended to thwart personal spiritual disciplines by encouraging careless comportment and by an overemphasis upon academic study at the expense of spiritual formation, and this when the schools ought to be "nurseries of the church for all estates" and "workshops of the Holy Spirit." Spener placed the chief burden upon the shoulders of professors. They should set a good example, exercise strict discipline among the students, and impress upon the students that "study without piety is worthless." Students cannot wait until they have been ordained and taken over their responsibilities as ministers to become pious persons. It would be most helpful, therefore, for professors to establish intimate friendships with students to be able to send them to their churches with testimonials regarding piety as well as diligence and skills. Tongue held slightly in cheek, Spener also proposed the renewed use of classics such as *The German Theology*; the sermons of John Tauler, "which, next to the Scriptures, probably made our dear Luther what he was" ; and *The Imitation of Christ*. He encouraged professors to reinstitute varied spiritual exercises— "how to institute pious meditations, how to know themselves better through self-examination, how to resist the lusts of the flesh, how to hold their desires in check and die unto the world . . . , how to observe growth in goodness or where there is still lack, and how they themselves may do what they must teach others to do." His considered judgment about the formation of the minister was that "a young man who fervently loves God, although adorned with limited gifts, will be more useful to the church of God with his meager talent and academic achievement than a vain and worldly fool with double doctor's degrees who is very clever but has not been taught by God."[14]

The Protestant seminary, born in the matrix of German Pietism, was in many respects a reaction to the failure of the universities to supply a well-rounded education for ministers, especially in regard to practical and spiritual aspects of their work. The seminary *per se* was a Roman Catholic creation. The Council of Trent had necessitated this when it declared that the training of the clergy thenceforth would take place in ecclesiastical institutions. It is easy to see why, then, Protestants established their seminaries with some reluctance. The oldest true Lutheran seminary was the one founded at Riddagshausen near Brunswick in 1690, which had clear if not formal connections with the Pietism of Spener.[15] A second was founded in Dresden in 1718, a third at Frankfurt in 1735. Anglicans tried early to establish theological colleges, but they did not survive, so that it was not until the nineteenth century that this movement caught on. In the United States the first seminaries were founded at the beginning of the nineteenth century; by midcentury there were more than fifty.

The rationalism of the Enlightenment probably spurred the widespread founding of seminaries for the training of ministers. During the eighteenth and nineteenth centuries, despite their inception in the church, the universities became increasingly secular. Their concern for academic exactitude

---

[14] Philip Jacob Spener, *Pia Desideria*, trans. and ed. Theodore G. Tappert (Philadelphia: Fortress Press, 1964), 103-15.
[15] So Ferdinand Cohrs, "Theological Education," *The New Schaff-Herzog Encyclopedia of Religious Knowledge*, XI:332.

tended to interfere with their devotion to the churches' aims and objectives. Seminaries, therefore, developed as institutions that would meet these aims without making apologies for their commitments. They fostered not only academic theology but also practical theology and spirituality.

Search for Wholistic Spiritual Formation

The last three or four decades have clouded the scene in education for Christian leadership in very much the same way the upheavals of the Renaissance and Reformation clouded it, and in the process they have left the matter of spiritual formation of ministers more crucial then ever. If sociological studies of recent years are right, we cannot expect neat and predictable patterns of church life in the future, for ours is an age of constant and rapidly accelerated change.

One change that impacts training of Christian leaders is a shift in the understanding of where ministry takes place. In the past, ministry was thought of as taking place mainly within the church buildings—in preaching, teaching, observing the sacraments, worship, and so on. Since World War II, however, critical world issues have gradually forced themselves more and more upon the churches' consciousness, so that now they are saying, "The kingdom of God and thus our ministry is in the world, in the secular city." Different theologies have justified and reinforced this confession. Radical theology in particular, taking its point of departure from Dietrich Bonhoeffer's *Letters and Papers from Prison*, denounced the churches' former complacency and "otherworldliness" and called for a positive embracing of the world in all of its unremitting secularity. The action is in the world, and if the churches want to be involved where the action is, they have to be in the world. Radical theology did not capture the fancy of everybody, but it made its mark. Even conservative Christians have recognized that the churches cannot live in ecclesiastical ghettoes of their own making.

If ministry is in the world, secular theologians also asked, where is the best place and what is the best way to train ministers? They answered, surely not in isolated enclaves that have little or nothing to do with the world. Training in monastic-type institutions, it was argued in the 1960s and 1970s, only heightens the widening chasm between the churches and the society of which they are a part. Ministers going from such enclaves to minister in the "real" world frequently suffer cultural shock and find themselves almost totally unprepared to cope with the urgent demands of their situations.

The theoretical answer to the question, Where is the best place to train persons for ministry? then, is "in the world, in the context of the jobs that they are going to perform." Such a conclusion is reinforced by the progressive philosophy of education and by the example of the early churches. Even colleges and universities are finding that they must broaden the locus of education, the whole world becoming, as it were, a workshop for learning.

In this context spiritual formation might seem to have lost a place entirely, for, in the minds of many, spiritual exercises and observances belong to the distinguishing and separating features of the church. In their desire to identify with the world and to minister to it, some radical theologians called for an abandonment of "churchy" practices. Correspondingly, ministers should surrender their sheltered and privileged station, perhaps take secular employment, and live like people of the world.

This line of reasoning offered a healthy corrective to the isolationist tendencies of the church, but it obviously went too far. Both theological and practical considerations press against it.

From a theological point of view, the churches have to decide whether or not they will seek to bring God as the

Ultimate Personal Reality in the universe into the picture of human experience, however much this may sometimes create a gap between the church and the world. The attempt to present to modern persons an expression of God that they can believe is highly commendable, but if that expression turns out to agree exactly with what they already believe, what in God's name do we have to offer anyway? I am inclined to agree with Thomas Merton, who was alluding to Karl Rahner's judgment, when he said that we Christians "have to make up our minds about our position in an unchristian world, a 'diaspora.' " Better to be one of a minority, even if that means a minority of one, than to affirm a secular person's faith on pretext of being "honest to God."[16]

From a practical standpoint, more careful reflection on the twentieth century causes many to conclude that it is highly questionable whether modern persons have become so mature and self-sufficient that they may toss all religious exercises out the window. At a superficial level the myth of modern persons "coming of age" has been shattered by widespread emotional problems, the abuse of drugs and alcohol, the consulting of horoscopes, the development of pseudoCults, the new interest in transcendental meditation, and other quasi-religious phenomena. At a deeper level, we may ask whether there is not some "ought" that compels human beings to seek God. Dietrich Bonhoeffer himself, for instance, spent about three hours daily in reading the Psalms, prayer, and other acts of devotion. Dag Hammarskjold, who appeared to the eyes of the world as a perfect specimen of the modern self-sufficient person, turned out to be a contemplative living and working in the world. Furthermore, we could compile a long list of those who today are asking whether we have not placed too much faith in ourselves, in our science, and in our technology, thus risking our very future.

---

[16] Thomas Merton, *Faith and Violence* (Notre Dame, Ind.: University of Notre Dame Press, 1968), 237.

Metahistorian Arnold Toynbee, among many others, remarked that humankind's only hope for survival depends on whether the great religions can lead us to rediscover the ground of our being. If these observations are true for humankind generally, are they not much more true for those who lead the churches? At a time when many within the world, within Western civilization, are looking for some kind of path that does not blend in with the rest of the maze, should the churches and their ministers erase every route sign? The answer to which many have been led in recent years is, Surely not! Rather, they have sought theological models by which those signs again appear intelligible. Good models have been offered by evolutionary or process theology, the theology of hope, and liberation theology, all of which affirm human life now but none of which forgets the ambiguities of it.

The issue, then, as construed on longer reflection, is not *whether* the churches shall have spiritual formation but how they shall pursue it. Vatican II directed that Roman Catholic clergy receive their spiritual formation in close conjunction with pastoral training. It reaffirmed many traditional features: the help of spiritual directors, the importance of eucharistic worship as the focus of the spiritual life, the intimate connection of priests with the bishop and the people, earnest practice of "those exercises of piety recommended by the venerable usage of the church," priestly poverty and celibacy. But it also showed an awareness of some new developments that affect the task of spiritual formation—notably "the latest findings in sound psychology and pedagogy." *The Decree on Priestly Formation* wedded both traditional and current language when it set as the goal of seminary training "a due degree of human maturity, attested chiefly by a certain emotional stability, by an ability to make considered decisions, and by a right manner of passing judgment on events and people."[17]

---

17 *Decree on Priestly Formation*, IV.11, in *The Documents of Vatican II*, ed. Walter M. Abbott, S.J. (New York: America Press, 1966), 448.

Protestants, especially those belonging to the Free Church tradition, have understandably moved more cautiously to program spiritual formation. This caution is a partial consequence of the Protestant Reformers' strictures against methods and techniques that imply a works salvation. Frequently, moreover, that caution relates to certain reservations and reactions to a superficial kind of pietism in their own heritage. The Protestant heritage has emphasized academic rather than personal formation. Only recently have Protestants begun seriously to take another look at the matter as Spener did in *Pia Desideria.*

Freed of many reservations by the improved ecumenical climate, Protestant seminaries have introduced many traditional elements of spiritual formation discarded at the Reformation. Whether they will transcend reservations concerning the use of means to effect spiritual growth and development will depend upon their integration into the total process of the formation of the minister as a person. To borrow a phrase from Father Camillus Ellspermann, O.S.B., Director of Formation at St. Meinrad School of Theology, the aim should be *"total* formation."[18] This means that instruction in spiritual formation may not be confined to worship experiences, a class on prayer, one-on-one spiritual direction, and other situations directed specifically to the "spiritual." The Jesuit paleontologist and philosopher Teilhard de Chardin, S.J., rightly reminded us that "by virtue of the Creation and, still more, of the Incarnation, *nothing* here below *is profane* to those who know how to see."[19] Accordingly, the Christian task is to divinize or sacralize all of life in Christ. Divinization takes place through your *activities* as well as through your passivities or symbolic acts of worship.

---

[18] Camillus Ellspermann, O.S.B., *"The Spiritual Formation of the Seminarian,"* paper delivered to the Faculty Colloquium of TEAM, October 20, 1969.
[19] Teilhard de Chardin, S.J., *Le Milieu Divin* (London: Fontana, 1964), 66.

Contrary to the view of some secular theologians, however, to see all of life as sacred and your task as one of divinization in Christ is not to negate the importance of symbolic acts of devotion. These principles imply that your acts of devotion should not take you *out of* the world but prepare you truly to enter it. For, to persons who believe that there is Divine Love at the heart of things, God "plucks the world out of our hearts" and simultaneously "hurls the world into our hearts, where we and [God] together carry it in infinitely tender love." [20] Your conscious acts of attentiveness to God sensitize you to the world and to people in the world.

The conclusion to which extensive reflection on the aim of total formation has led many is that the burden for spiritual formation falls upon the total educational experience in which Christian leaders are involved. A report of the American Association of Theological Schools concluded that a student "*is being spiritually formed or malformed*" in his or her "*experience of the entire spectrum of seminary life.*" In a manner reminiscent of Spener's *Pia Desideria*, it proceeded to place the burden for spiritual formation upon the faculty: "*If any one thing has emerged from our study of seminaries, it is the conviction that the spiritual development and formation of students begins with and depends on the spirituality of the faculty.*"[21]

---

[20] Thomas R. Kelly, *A Testament of Devotion* (London: Hodder & Stoughton, 1941), 43f.
[21] *Theological Education 8* (Spring 1972): 179.

Conclusion

All Christians have done much to get anchored in the mainstream of Christian spirituality in the last forty years. The churches have not found a magic formula for spiritual formation. However, rediscovery of the churches' ancient stores of wisdom in the "New Pentecost" of Pope John XXIII offers some hope that we can move into the future with some assurance about spiritual formation of Christian leaders for an age of challenge and hope. I hope that you will continue to grow spiritually as you meet the new challenges and opportunities before you.

Chapter 3

THE MAIN THING: A RELATIONSHIP WITH GOD

The central concern of a Christian leader should be the same as that of every Christian, namely, an intimate personal relationship with God. You want to *know* God, to partake of the life of God, not just know *about* God. The ancient psalmist declared,

> As a deer longs for flowing streams,
>   so my soul longs for you, O God.
> My soul thirsts for God,
>   for the living God. (Ps. 42:1-2)

How does such a relationship develop? "Very much as you cultivate an intimate relationship with another human being," the saints of Christian history have said. "Through communion, communication, or conversation, getting to know one another. That is what prayer is."

The Two Motions of Prayer

I think of prayer in essence as having two motions. *The first motion is one of response.* It is opening like a flower opening to the morning sunshine to allow God's love energies to flow into your inner chamber. You may know that many flowers close up at night, folding their petals in. When it begins to become daylight, they open just a little. Then as the sun's rays strike them, they open a little more and a little more until they are wide open.

"God is love," an apostle writes (1 John 4:8). Theologically, you must say, God's love energies brought the world into being. God's love energies sustain the world. God's love energies are directing the world toward some meaningful end. And the same love energies are constantly pouring on you. That is true even though you cannot see God in the same way that the sun's energy is bathing the earth even when you cannot see it, when it is on the other side of the earth. Were that not true, you would be a block of ice.

God, you see, is the initiator of this communion. If you will think about it a moment, you will quickly realize why that is true. Physicists today are pointing out that our sun is one of millions of suns in our galaxy and our galaxy is one of more than 150 billion galaxies. Our God is a God of 150 billion-plus galaxies! And when I think about that, my mouth gapes open in awe.

Yet God's greatness is not the most awesome discovery. The most awesome is what we learn from revelation—that the God of 150 billion-plus galaxies cares about me, about you, grains of sand on an endless seashore. That, you see, is what the whole of revelation tells us, that God, the God of this vast universe, loves us with an infinite love. "While we were still sinners, Christ died for us. That proves God's love," the Apostle Paul put it (Rom. 5:8, author's translation). There is great truth in the much-loved spiritual: "[God's] got the whole world in [God's] hands. . . . [God's] got you and me, brother . . . sister, in [God's] hands. [God's] got the whole world in [God's] hands."

Had God not sought us, you and I could not shout loud enough, put up long enough antennae, or send out a spaceship far enough to get God's attention. Rufus Jones spoke of "the double search." God has made us so that by nature we seek the Other because God seeks us. The human heart responds to God, Jones has said, as naturally as the retina of the eye responds to light waves. Or, to change the analogy, the heart makes its way toward God as naturally as the homing instinct of the pigeon takes it to the place of its birth. "You have made us for Yourself," Augustine prayed at the beginning of his Confessions, "and our heart is restless until it finds rest in you."[1]

All of this makes it sound very easy. "Just open. Just let love flow in." But you know it is not that easy to open. You have experienced "storms" in life that have caused you to pull your shutters to and bar your door from the inside. After you have experienced one of those "storms," it's not so easy to open again. You're afraid that it might be still raging, that it might come back.

I'm not speaking as much about the physical storms as I am psychic "storms" that cause you to clam up. You make yourself vulnerable by loving another person. That person spurns, exploits, twists, distorts your love. Surely no human experience causes greater pleasure or pain than love. Some never risk intimate relationships at all because they cannot handle such intense suffering. They draw back into a cocoon. Life hands out a lot of "cold pricklies." Sad to say, even the church, put on earth to increase love of God and of neighbor, hands out a lot of "cold pricklies." When you experience them, it is not easy to open.

---

[1] Augustine *Confessions* 1.1 (author's translation).

Something else that makes it hard to open to God is the need to merit whatever you receive. As I grew up in poverty in the Missouri Ozarks during the Great Depression, my mother drilled into me that, if I wanted to have any pride and self-esteem, I should never accept anything free. Her principle was in many ways a gift for which I am grateful. There is a genuine and necessary pride that all human beings need. But my mother also left me with a problem, the problem of accepting grace. I don't believe I accepted a piece of candy from another person until I was twenty-five. Saliva sometimes dripped out the corner of my mouth, but I would still say, "Oh, no, thank you. I've just had some." Or "I'm about to have lunch. I'd better not take any now."

George Herbert, the great Anglican pastor and poet, put his finger on the problem in a part of his poem on the church:

> Love bade me welcome: yet my soul drew back,
>   Guilty of dust and sin.
> But quick-ey'd Love, observing me grow slack,
>   From my first entrance in,
> Drew nearer to me, sweetly questioning,
>   If I lacked any thing.
>
> A guest, I answer'd, worthy to be here:
>   Love said, You shall be he.
> I the unkind, the ungrateful? Ah my dear,
>   I cannot look on thee.
> Love gently took my hand, and smiling did reply,
>   Who made the eyes but I?[2]

God, Divine Love, is always carrying on a love affair, trying to

---

[2] *George Herbert*, "Love" from *The Temple in The Works of George Herbert in Prose and Verse Vol. II* (London: Bell and Daldy, 1859), 217-218.

woo you to Godself. But you have to open, from the inside. God does not drive a bulldozer.

Spiritual growth and development depend on this opening to let God's love come in. If you can open just a crack, that love will come in, drive out your fear, and still your anxieties. As a child, I was always astonished at what I saw natural daylight do. If there was a slit in the shade, a crack under the door, or just the keyhole, when day dawned, the light would come in and refract throughout the entire room until it illuminated everything. God's love works that way in your inner life. It squeezes in through the tiniest of openings, refracts throughout your entire inner self, and drives out the fear and anxieties that prevent you from becoming who you are.

The author of 1 John said, "Perfect love casts out fear." Perfect love means *God's* love, the Love God is. Fear is natural to human beings, and it plays an important positive role in life. But fear carried to excess is disabling and destructive. Such fear keeps you from opening to God or to others. It prevents you from realizing your potential as a human being. It withers your mind, heart, and soul. But if you can open just a slit, Love will come in and drive out the fear that immobilizes and paralyzes you and keeps you from being the person you can be, the person you truly are.

In thoughts reminiscent of Jesus' teaching in Matthew 6:25-34, the Apostle Paul noted how Love can also help you to overcome anxiety, fear's blood brother. Anxiety, too, is natural to human beings. It supplies motivation for much human activity. Yet anxiety or worry also has a downside. If it is excessive, it diminishes you. To the anxiety-ridden, therefore, Paul says, "Stop worrying about everything. Rather, in every circumstance in prayer and entreaty with thanksgiving let your requests be made known to God, and the *shalom* of God, which surpasses all human comprehension, will throw a cordon of troops around your hearts and your minds in Christ Jesus" (Phil.

4:5-7, AP). I used the Hebrew word *shalom* here because it means more than the English word peace usually suggests in our culture. In this beautifully picturesque passage, Paul is talking about a deep down security that only God can give to still anxiety or worry.

"We are put on earth a little space that we may learn to bear the beams of love," William Blake wrote. You have to *learn*. It won't happen automatically. Self-consciously, you might try things that will help you to open that tiny crack to let God's love energies flow in to overwhelm fears and anxieties.

The other motion of prayer is one in which you become a *transmitter of God's love energies*. Ideally, you should become, as it were, a *step-up* transmitter. Step-down transformers reduce electric current from 220 to 110. When I have gone to Europe, I have usually taken one in order to use American-made appliances. In the 1960s that was a box weighing about fifteen pounds; today it is a small three-inch cube that plugs into a socket. There are also step-up transformers. To increase the current, you have to add electrical energy. To become a step-up transmitter of God's love energies, you as a human being made in the image of God would need to let God's love energies flow through you in your prayers and work and to add some of your own love energies to God's.

To be a good conduit of divine love energies requires transparency. Many things can impede the flow of love. One of these is anger. Anger is a very powerful emotion, perhaps next to love the most powerful of all. That is why the desert fathers and mothers spent much time discussing how to get it out of the way. In that they learned much from the Psalms of the Hebrew Bible. They learned that it is all right to show anger, even at God.

Most psalms are what are called "laments" or "complaints." From them you learn how transparency contributes to intimacy. The psalmists "let their hair down" before God. They had entered into a covenant with God, like a marriage covenant. They had a right and an obligation to hold God accountable just as God had to hold them accountable.

Especially revealing among the laments are the group called "imprecatory" psalms, the ones that call on God to curse people.

> O God, break the teeth in their mouths;
> tear out the fangs of the young lions, O Lord!
> Let them vanish like water that runs away;
> like grass let them be trodden down and wither.
> Let them be like the snail that dissolves into slime;
> like the untimely birth that never sees the sun.
> (Ps. 58:6-8)

Now that psalmist was mad, and he did not try to hide it.

Many Christians have not known what to do with such psalms. Scholars have half-seriously suggested making a condensation and leaving out the imprecatory psalms. How could such hymns of hate have gotten in the Bible? Can they be reconciled with the teaching of Jesus about love of enemies? I was among those who did not appreciate those psalms until, pummeled by critics, I discovered a recurrent line in them, "Vengeance is mine, I will repay, says the Lord," quoted also by Paul in Romans 12:19. In my situation that psalm offered clear counsel. Let your anger off to God. God can handle it. The people you are mad at cannot. And you cannot retain the anger. If you bottle it up inside, anger will become a volcano. Sometimes the best prayer you can pray is to go into your closet and cuss.

Too often you have been warned against presenting yourself to God just as you are. You are taught early a conventional dishonesty with God, such as, "When you pray, put a smile on your face. Be nice. You might offend God. Don't let God know how you really feel." The psalmists insist that if you really want to have an intimate relationship with God, then come to the relationship as you are. Do not wear a mask. God can handle you without any cosmetics.

If you get such things as anger and frustration out of the way, then you can take in love energies and let them flow through you into your activities and toward other persons. You should recognize, of course, that you will still vary in your conduction. Sometimes you will take in 2,000 volts and consume all of it in your being transformed. Other times you will take in 2,000 and out will come 1 volt. Still other times you will take in 2,000 and out will come 6, enough to light up a small flashlight bulb. Now and then, you may let those energies flow through you unimpeded and add to them some energies you have generated, thus becoming a step-up transmitter.

Ultimately, the key lies with the first motion, responding to God's prior initiative. Long before you have your first thought about prayer, God has been trying to get your attention, to engage you in a vital communion. Your first need is to pay attention. Prayer is, above all, attentiveness to God.

In *Beginning to Pray* Archbishop Anthony Bloom recounts how, when he was sent to a home for the aging shortly after his ordination as a priest, a 102-year-old woman came to him to get help with a problem in prayer.

He replied, "Oh yes, ask So-and-so."

She said, "All these years I have been asking people who are reputed to know about prayer, and they have never given me a sensible reply, so I thought that as you probably know nothing, you may by chance blunder out the right thing."

With that wonderful compliment, he asked, "What is your problem?"

She said, "These fourteen years I have been praying the Jesus prayer almost continually, and never have I experienced God's presence at all."

So Bloom "blundered out" what he thought. "If you

speak all this time, you don't give God a chance to place a word in."

When she asked what she should do, he directed, "Go to your room after breakfast, put it right, place your armchair in a strategic position that will leave behind your back all the dark corners which are always in an old lady's room into which things are pushed so as not to be seen. Light your little lamp before the ikon that you have and first of all take stock of your room. Just sit, look round, and try to see where you live, because I am sure that if you have prayed all these fourteen years it is a long time since you have seen your room. And then take your knitting and for fifteen minutes knit before the face of God, but I forbid you to say one word of prayer. You just knit and try to enjoy the peace of your room."

She was very skeptical but agreed to do it. After a while, she returned and said, "You know, it works!"

He asked, "What works?" He had never advised anyone to do that before and was curious to find out what did work.

She explained that she had followed his advice to the letter. She set her room in order and then settled into her armchair. As she looked around her room, she said, "Goodness, what a nice room I live in." She felt quiet and peaceful. She noticed the clock ticking, but that was not distracting. It just deepened the silence. Her needles bumped the arms of the chair, but that was not distracting either. Then she noticed that the silence had substance. "It was not the absence of something but presence of something. The silence had a density, a richness, and it began to pervade me," she said. "The silence around began to come and meet the silence in me." Then she added, "All of a sudden I perceived that the silence was a presence."[3]

---

3 Archbishop Anthony Bloom, *Beginning to Pray* (New York: Paulist Press, 1970), 92-93. I have taken the liberty of arranging the dialogue.

Praying Without Ceasing

The goal of Christians throughout history has been to fulfill 1 Thessalonians 5:17, "Pray without ceasing." They have tried different approaches. In early centuries some disciples went to the desert and went without sleep in order to fulfill this commission. They called themselves *Akoimitai*, "the nonsleepers." Some prayed all 150 Psalms every day. In those days, of course, they had to memorize the Psalms, for individuals could rarely own Bibles or even parts of Bibles. They were hand copied.

Others developed "the prayer of the heart," the official prayer of Orthodox Christians: "Lord Jesus Christ, Son of God, have mercy on me, a sinner," or abbreviated forms of those words. The object was to be ever conscious of the presence of the risen Christ. In more recent times a Russian Orthodox Christian, studying writings of the desert fathers and mothers, came up with a formula for developing prayer of the heart and recorded it in *The Way of the Pilgrim*. The first week pray the formula 3,000 times a day, the second week 6,000, the third week 12,000, synchronizing the syllables with your heartbeat. Ever after, the unnamed author assured, whether you were awake or asleep, your heart would be beating those words.

Some have found more helpful the approach of a seventeenth-century Carmelite lay brother named Nicholas Herman known as Brother Lawrence. Brother Lawrence was a simple person. After serving in the army during the Thirty Years' War, he was mustered out and was a footman for a French noble family. He then entered a Carmelite monastery in midlife. For the first ten years in the monastery, he tried the rigorous disciplines of the order, but they only frustrated him. One day, washing dishes in the kitchen, he discovered that he could talk to the God of pots and pans, or as he phrased it in the title of that little classic, he could "practice the presence of God." In whatever he was doing, he said, he maintained an attitude of attention to the presence. Brother Lawrence had a passionate regard for God. "I turn my little omelette in the pan for love of God," he said. He fell head over heels in love with God and let that transfuse and transform everything he did. You know what happens when you are head over heels in love. You can't get the beloved out of your mind. The beloved is a presence in everything at every moment.

To love God like that, Brother Lawrence went on to say, you have to get to know God, and getting to know God requires paying attention. If you learn how to "see" and to "listen," you can make all of life a prayer. "Seeing" here means more than looking, viewing the outside. To paraphrase George Herbert, you "may look on glass and stay the eye," or, if you please, "through it pass, and thus the heaven espy." To those who know how to "see," Teilhard de Chardin has said so aptly, "nothing here below is secular." Everything has been made sacred in its origins by God, and everything will be divinized.[4]

Scriptures remind you that God has built messages into the order of things or is always beaming messages to you. God beams messages to you through nature, through history, and through your life. *First, through nature.* Psalm 19 makes a bold declaration:

> The heavens are telling the glory of God;
>> and the firmament proclaims [God's] handiwork.
> Day to day pours forth speech,
>> and night to night declares knowledge.

The psalmist recognized, as you would, that this is not a matter of physical sound.

> There is no speech, nor are there words;

---

[4] Pierre Teilhard de Chardin, *The Divine Milieu* (New York: Harper & Brothers, 1960), 15, 30, 33.

their voice is not heard;
yet their voice goes out through all the earth,
and their words to the end of the world. (Ps. 19:1-4)
The familiar Psalm 8 invites you to open yourself:
O Lord, our Sovereign, how majestic is your name in all
the earth! . . .
When I look at your heavens, the work of your fingers,
the moon and the stars that you have established;
[then I must ask,]
what are human beings that you are mindful of them,
mortals that you care for them? (Ps. 8:1, 3-4)

You know, too, how often Jesus used nature to teach
about God. The lilies of the field, the birds of the air, the hairs of
your head—all remind you how intimately God is involved in
your life, how much God cares (Matt. 6:25-34; Luke 12:22-32).
Within nature is a story, and if you will come as a little child and
enter into the story in imagination, it will open up insight about
God, about God's care, about life, about the world, about you.

Second, God beams messages through history. That is
true of *all* history because God is Lord of all history. The
Egyptian, the Babylonian, the Assyrian, the Persian stories all
left evidence of God's tracks in history. Cyrus, the Persian king,
could be called "the Lord's anointed." But God's self-revelation
occurs especially in particular segments of history, in a story of
stories.

For the Jewish people the story of stories is the exodus
from Egypt. Jews gather at Passover time to remember and
relive the exodus in what they call a home *seder.* According to
instructions of Jesus' day recorded in the *Mishnah*, the *seder*
was to be observed in this way. After a meal of lamb and herbs,
the youngest child was to ask, "Why is this night different from
all other nights?" Then the head of the family was to recount the
story of the exodus from Egypt. Then the instructions added,

"Do this as if you yourselves were going out in the exodus from Egypt." In other words, come like the child who asked the question and enter into the story in imagination and let the story do a job on you.

For a Christian there's another story of stories, the story of Jesus—his life, his death, and his resurrection. It is not by chance that Christian meditation has focused on the Gospels. The whole of scriptures is important. They tell the larger story. But it is especially in the story of Jesus that God's self-disclosure reaches its peak. If you will come as a little child and enter into the story, it will illuminate and transform you.

What do you want to happen? The Apostle Paul gives the answer to that in Philippians 2:5: "Let the same mind be in you that was in Christ Jesus." He does not leave to your guessing what that mind would be. He gives the good news in a thimble. God loved humankind so much that God shared the pain and shame and ignominy of human life—even death—in and through Jesus of Nazareth to disclose life's ultimate end and goal, its hope. As Paul wrote in Romans 5:8, "While we were still sinners, Christ died for us. That proves God's love" (author's translation). Hearing that, not just as words or thoughts, but taking it existentially into the very center of your being, will transform your life. God says, "I love you with an infinite and incomprehensible love."

You can see in all of this how the Hebrew way of knowing differed from the Greek way of knowing. The Greek way, which has come down to us in the form of scientific thinking, was the way of empirical observation and rational reflection. You look with your eyes, listen with your ears, touch, taste, and smell; then you reflect rationally upon the evidence. The Hebrew way was the way of story. In nature is a story. In history is a story. In your own life is a story. And if you will come like a child and enter into the story in imagination, the story will shape and mold you.

Observe here the importance of imagination. Is it not imagination that sets a child apart? Have you watched children as they listen to a good storyteller? They reply to questions that weren't asked. They act out parts of the story. *That* story becomes *their* story. Perhaps that is what Jesus meant when he said, "Unless you become as little children, you shall not enter the kingdom of God."

Stories have shaped some of your deepest perceptions. Who you are, the way you act, your outlook on life have been molded by some stories much more than by discursive reason. I know that is true in my case. The values I treasure, the outlook I have, the way I go about making decisions result from the imprints of stories that are etched on my very being, stories spun out in the lives of parents, teachers, friends, public leaders.

Do you know Nathaniel Hawthorne's *The Great Stone Face*?[5] The story is about a boy named Ernest, who, in a natural outcropping of rock on the face of a cliff near his home, saw a Great Stone Face. He heard again and again the Native American legend that one day a child would be born in the valley who, when grown to manhood, would bear the exact likeness of the Great Stone Face. All of his life, he cherished the legend and meditated on that face. He saw there lines of wisdom, truth, and love. Throughout his life he asked, "Who is that Great Stone Face?" He was disappointed when he did not see the face in a rich man, a famous soldier, a statesman, or even a poet whose poetry hymned the qualities in that Great Stone Face. As an older man, Ernest introduced the poet to the people of his village. Then the poet told the assembly that the Great Stone Face was *Ernest*! He had become what he had spent his life contemplating.

---

[5] This classic has recently been republished in an abridged and illustrated version. Nathaniel Hawthorne, *The Great Stone Face*, abridged by Penelope J. Stokes (Colorado Springs, Colo.: Chariot Victor Publishing, 1997).

If you have allowed the story of stories to saturate your life, then as you go through life, you can *listen to your life.* Michel Quoist has shown how to do that in his wonderful collection entitled *Prayers.* If you knew how to look at life through God's eyes, if you knew how to listen to God in all of life, he says, all of life would become a prayer. A twenty-dollar bill, the sea, a pornographic magazine, eyes, a wire fence, a youth brought in with an overdose of drugs, a drunk in the middle of the street, a hospital—everything, a prayer.

Douglas V. Steere, one of the leading Quakers of the twentieth century, was a mentor and teacher in the spiritual life for many. A Harvard Ph.D. and a Rhodes Scholar at Oxford, he spent much of his life in a quest to know God. At Harvard he discovered the reality and centrality of prayer. Everywhere he traveled, he drank eagerly of the wisdom of others on the spiritual life and spent his life encouraging "the intensification of the life of God in the individual hearts of men [and women]" [6] Most of his writings had something to do with the spiritual life.[7]

In his classic *On Listening to Another*[8] Douglas Steere has listed four qualities of a good listener. The first is **vulnerability**. Vulnerability comes from the Latin words meaning "capable of being wounded," "able to be hurt." Douglas reminds how much better the people with leprosy on the island of Molokai in Hawaii heard Father Damien that morning he began his sermon, "Brothers, we lepers." And, I should add, how much better Damien heard them after he contracted leprosy!

The second is **acceptance**. This does not mean, Douglas

---

[6] Douglas V. Steere, *On Beginning from Within* (New York: Harper & Brothers, 1943), vii.

[7] For the fuller story see E. Glenn Hinson, *Love at the Heart of Things: A Biography of Douglas V. Steere* (Wallingford, Penn.: Pendle Hill Publications; Nashville, Tenn: Upper Room Books, 1998).

[8] Douglas V. Steere, *On Listening to Another* (New York: Harper & Brothers, 1955), 20-24.

says, toleration born of indifference. Acceptance comes very close to what agape-love means in the New Testament. Agape is the kind of love that does not try to shape and mold the other person into its own mold. It accepts the other just as that person is.

The third is **expectancy**. Expectancy has to do with hopefulness. Douglas Steere was the kind of person who inspired hope in others. Many are those who would say that, until Alzheimer's disease impaired his faculties, they never met Douglas without feeling buoyed up and encouraged. In writing his biography I spent much time trying to discover the secret behind such experiences. I found two clues.

One is an optimism that pervaded his life. He could always see a ray of light penetrating every dark cloud. He looked at life from the bright side. Teilhard de Chardin possessed that same optimism grounded in a conviction that God, Divine Love, is at the very heart of things. "We must overcome death," he said, "by finding God in it."[9] Yes. That is true. And I could go on to add, "We overcome sickness, we overcome grief, we overcome life by finding God in it."

The other is a sense of mission Douglas Steere had. It was something he learned from Martin Buber in a Quaker meeting at Haverford College in 1951. During the meeting, the remarkable Jewish philosopher said that the greatest thing one person could do for another was to confirm what was deepest in the other. That thought constantly recurred in Douglas's speech and writing, but more important, it pervaded his relationships with others. He wanted, above everything, to confirm what was deepest in other persons, arousing the hope that was in them.

The fourth is **constancy**. The Latin and Greek behind this word mean "to stand with" or "stay with" another. Douglas speaks of "infinite patience." Really to listen to another, you have to exercise patience. You can't "ho hum" and start saying, "Oh, you mean . . ." when you don't know what someone means but are saying, "If you will say something like this, we can get on with this and I can go on to something else." To listen is to "stay with" the other.

Listening is more than hearing words and distinguishing sounds. Seeing is more than looking at objects. Douglas Steere cited a story from John Woolman, the eighteenth-century Quaker saint. Following a Native American rebellion, Woolman undertook a dangerous trip to visit the Delaware Indians at Wehaloosing on the Susquehanna River. Initially, he tried to communicate with their chief, Papunehang, through a Moravian missionary. When that seemed unsuccessful, he asked the interpreters to let him pray without translation. Before the meeting closed, he was told that Papunehang had said, "I love to feel where words come from."[10] The object is to get beyond words and thoughts. Communication has many levels, and you want to reach the deepest of them.

Within every exchange, moreover, there is more than the speaker and the hearer. There is also the Eternal Listener, Kierkegaard's Eternal Spectator. God is there. Douglas Steere cited Psalm 139, that wonderful poem about God's inescapable nearness. In the first seven verses the psalmist told how intimately God knows each person: "Even before a word is on my tongue, O Lord, you know it completely" (v. 4). Then in verse 8, this one who wanted so desperately to escape God summed up his experience of God's unavoidable presentness: "If I ascend to heaven, you are there." That, of course, is where you expect God to be. But the other half, "if I make my bed in Sheol, you are there," that is what rolls over you.

Two things in that jump out at you. First, the psalmist said, "If I *make* my bed," not if I trip and fall in. You can't mess up your life so badly that God will not be there. Second, Sheol is

---

10 John Woolman, *The Journal of John Woolman* (New York: Corinth Books, 1961), 151.

by definition in Hebrew thought where God is not. But for our psalmist there is nowhere God is not.

> If I take the wings of the morning
> and settle at the farthest limits of the sea,
> even there your hand shall lead me,
> and your right hand shall hold me fast.
> If I say, "Surely the darkness shall cover me,
> and the light around me become night,"
> even the darkness is not dark to you;
> the night is as bright as the day,
> for darkness is as light to you. (vv. 9-12)

What do you do with your listening and your seeing? Douglas Steere contends that, if you really listen, you may listen another person to a condition of awareness of the Eternal Listener's presence. And if you really listen, you may become aware of the Eternal Listener.

Improving Your Attentiveness to God

Having said all of this, I believe we must recognize that we are not doing very well with our seeing and our listening in our age and culture. We see but do not perceive. We hear but do not listen.

One facet of our problem, surely, is our busyness. We get caught up in activity for activity's sake. We run pantingly and frantically through crowded calendars. For many, not just activity but *quantity* of activity determines how we feel about ourselves. And in our hurried and harried lives, we do not take time for other persons or, more seriously, for the Ultimate Personal Reality in the universe.

Another side to this is distractedness. We live in a very

distracted and distracting culture. The noise level alone is enough to overtax our systems. Add to that the glut of sights and demands vying for our attention, and it is easy to see why we risk what Alvin Toffler called "future shock." Future shock is something like the battle fatigue soldiers on the front lines experience. We reach a point where we can no longer process and respond to what is happening around us.

I wonder if our busyness and our distractedness are not to a great extent responsible for something else that is happening in our society, an escalation of violence or aggressiveness and a failure to come to the aid of others. Who today remembers the name of Kitty Genovese? She was the New York woman murdered in broad daylight while forty people watched. No one turned a hand to help as she broke free from her assailant three times and cried for help. When that incident happened, many people decried that horrible event and the passivity of those who witnessed it. Now we all witness greater horrors on entertainment programs and accept them as normative.

The key question for you, therefore, may be: How do you improve your listening and seeing and feeling? In Christian history there have been two recommendations, polar opposites of each other. One is to spend time with people who are hurting. When Evelyn Underhill, a brilliant student and already widely recognized scholar in Christian mysticism, sought Baron von Hugel as her spiritual guide, he told her to go first and spend two afternoons a week in the ghetto. "It will, if properly entered into and persevered with," he explained, "discipline, mortify, deepen and quiet you. It will, as it were, distribute your blood—some of your blood—away from your brain, where too much is lodged at present." [11]

---

[11] Cited by Margaret Cropper, *Life of Evelyn Underhill* (New York: Harper & Brothers, Publishers, 1958), 75.

You must recognize, however, that you cannot stand an uninterrupted exposure to pain and suffering. That, too, can desensitize and harden you to others' hurt. For instance, you watch the massacre of innocents in Rwanda or Serbia, the starving of millions in Ethiopia, the latest "ethnic cleansing" or genocide on CNN. The first week sickens and fills you with resolve to do something. But by the second week you throw up your hands and exclaim, "Oh, no! Not that again!"

That is why you have the opposite proposal: Spend time in solitude and silence. Solitude permits you to retreat from the press and struggle in order to let your fragmented and dispersed self become collected. That is the purpose of a retreat. The word re-treat means "drawing back." In the busy and distracting culture you would do well to have a daily retreat, thirty minutes just "wasting time for God"; an all-day monthly retreat; and at least one or two thirty-six-to forty-eight-hour retreats every year. Solitude will get you away from busyness and distractedness long enough to permit you to be re-created.

Silence goes hand in hand with solitude. Silence sensitizes, just as noise desensitizes. Some early Christians sought solitude and silence in the desert. When Basil Pennington came to lecture at Wake Forest University, my wife and I took him to a favorite restaurant located in a busy shopping mall. After we had eaten, we came out to the parking lot. Basil stopped, held up his hand, and said, "I hear a katydid." Not another person there heard a katydid, but Basil spends most of his time in silence.

To see and to listen. In *A Testament of Devotion* Thomas Kelly wrote about living life on two levels. One is the level of activities. Some people live life only on that level. They have nothing deeper to inform what they are doing. But there is another level on which you may live life. That is the level of the interior life—of communion, communication, conversation with God. When you first become serious about your relationship with God, Kelly observes, you may alternate between those two. But as you grow and develop, you may do them simultaneously. Not now one and now the other, but while you are engaged in activities, quietly, behind the scenes as it were, you carry on your secret communion. In a similar approach to the spiritual journey, Dietrich Bonhoeffer required the seminarians at the Confessing Church's seminary at Finkenwalde to spend thirty minutes every morning meditating on the same passage of scriptures for a week. The rest of the day, they were to work. And in the it of work, Bonhoeffer explained, you may find the Thou of God. All of life becomes your prayer.

Chapter 4

HOLDING YOURSELF ACCOUNTABLE

Really serious commitment to your friendship with God requires some ways to hold yourself accountable. Because God does not shout, scream, or jump up and down to get your attention, you have to carry more of the responsibility for keeping the friendship alive. Do not imagine that you, as a religious leader, will have fewer spiritual difficulties than others because you are engaged in "God's business."

Religious professionals may run greater risks than ordinary saints. All too readily, caught up in the affairs of religion, they begin to turn it into a performance, a role, an act, and push their personal relationship with God to the side. Just as Jesus warned (Matt. 6:5-6), they become hypocrites, "play actors" who make sure everyone sees how devout they are and what they are doing. In the meantime, such leaders dry up inwardly and have nothing to offer the world that the world does not already have in abundance. As another early Christian observed, they have the *form* of religion but not its *power* (2 Tim. 3:5).

Different persons will have diverse ways of assuring accountability. Most religious orders have required individual spiritual guides. Ignatius Loyola considered such guides mandatory for persons doing the *Spiritual Exercises*.[1] The Roman Catholic Church has not mandated individual spiritual directors for all members, but from about the early Middle Ages, the church has required regular confession to priests. When the Protestant Reformers rejected both the monastic model and the practice of oral confession, they placed accountability for the covenant with God on the individual. We call this the doctrine of the priesthood of all believers. People did not need another person looking out for their relationship with God. They could handle that themselves.

The Protestant approach did not work out in practice as well as it seemed to promise in theory. Perhaps we could say that spiritually, the Protestant faithful were quick to take the bus and leave the driving up to Jesus! Behind the problem lay perhaps an inadequate definition of grace, one emphasizing God's acquittal of the sinner at the Judgment rather than God's gift of Godself, the Spirit, to foster growth in the relationship with God. As a means of attaining accountability, John Calvin framed the Ecclesiastical Ordinances of Geneva, which legislated penalties for failure to practice proper piety. Puritanism followed in his train, emphasizing especially Sabbath observance. The Puritan experiment in New England, however, proved that the churches cannot legislate faithfulness. By the third generation church attendance had dwindled to about 6 percent of the population.

The Great Awakening pumped new life into moribund religion between 1720 and 1760 and also fostered a more experiential approach to religion. The American colonies benefited from the advent of Pietism via the Moravians and Methodism. Pietism and Methodism emphasized holiness or

---

[1] Ignatius Loyola, *The Spiritual Exercises and Selected Works*, edited by George E. Ganss, Classics of Western Spirituality (New York: Paulist Press, 1991).

sanctification fostered in "schools of piety" or "class meetings" where people could share in more intimate ways and thus hold one another accountable. In 1675 Philip Jacob Spener had made earnest Bible study in small cell groups the first item in his plan for revitalizing the Lutheran Church in Germany.[2] John Wesley, who became acquainted with Moravians on his mission to Georgia and participated for a time in a Moravian Society, adapted the cell group idea in the Wesleyan revival.

Another way of keeping tabs on your relationship with God is journal keeping. Journal keeping has a long heritage in Christianity. Women, incidentally, deserve considerable credit for the practice. Perpetua, a Carthaginian noblewoman put to death for her faith while still a catechumen around 200, kept a "Diary" of her experience in prison, including very personal dreams and accounts of her interaction with her captors and her family.[3] Egeria, a Spanish nun, penned a remarkably detailed account of a pilgrimage to Egypt and the Holy Land in 383.[4] Many medieval women of the thirteenth through fifteenth centuries recorded deeply personal experiences of "revelations." Since the Reformation of the sixteenth century, both Protestants and Catholics have journaled as a means of deepening their engagement with God. Puritans such as John Bunyan[5] often

---

[2] Philip Jacob Spener, *Pia Desideria*, trans. and ed. Theodore G. Tappert (Philadelphia: Fortress Press, 1964), 87-92.

[3] Perpetua's "Diary" composes the body of *The Martyrdom of Saints Perpetua and Felicitas*. A reliable contemporary text and translation is found in *The Acts of the Christian Martyrs*, trans. Herbert Musurillo (Oxford: Clarendon Press, 1972).

[4] See *Egeria's Travels*, trans. John Wilkinson (London: SPCK, 1971). Her name is also given as Etheria.

[5] John Bunyan, *Grace Abounding to the Chief of Sinners*, 1. *The Pilgrim's Progress* is, at least in part, a symbolic presentation of the struggle recorded by Bunyan in *Grace Abounding*. (See Doubleday Devotional Classics, edited by E. Glenn Hinson. Garden City, NY: Doubleday & Co., Inc., 1978.) For other Puritan journals see Owen C. Watkins, *The Puritan Experience* (London: Routledge and Kegan Paul, 1972).

kept careful accounts of "the working of grace" in their lives. In the American colonies David Brainerd recorded in minute detail in his Diary[6] his awareness of the operation of grace as he witnessed the conversion of Native Americans during the peak years of the Great Awakening. Jonathan Edwards, whose daughter cared for Brainerd as he lay dying of tuberculosis, turned the Diary into a classic of Christian devotion. Quakers from the time of George Fox[7] made the journal a mainstay for tracking their devotion as well as an instrument of witness to others. John Woolman used his Journal [8] to get across to others some of his ideas about overcoming oppression and injustice, especially in the slave trade. John Wesley[9] kept a detailed account of his spiritual life from his "holy club" days at Oxford followed by his mission to the American colonies in 1735.

What Is a Journal?

Since the rest of this chapter will focus on journaling, I want to define journal more closely. Although some journals have been labeled diaries, journals—at least those devoted to spiritual growth—differ from diaries. They are not simply reports or log books on the day's activities, even if such things are included. Journals are concerned more with inner than with outer readings.

---

[6] *The Life and Diary of David Brainerd*, ed. Jonathan Edwards (Chicago: Moody Press, 1949).

[7] *The Journal of George Fox* was compiled by Thomas Ellwood rather than Fox. A good modern edition has been done by John L. Nickalls (Cambridge, Eng.: Cambridge University Press, 1952).

[8] Woolman used a selective approach to his journal to present himself as a model for social action, especially on the issue of slavery. See *The Journal and Major Essays of John Woolman*, ed. Phillips P. Moulton (New York: Oxford University Press, 1971).

[9] John Wesley, *Journal,* edited by Nehemiah Curnock, 8 vols. (London: Epworth Press, 1938).

In the deepest sense perhaps they record conversation, communication, communion with God. Described in this way, an enduring classic such as Augustine's *Confessions* would come very close to the journal category. Morton Kelsey has remarked, "The goal here is not simply that of achieving my own potential, but rather of deepening my relationship with that center of spiritual reality of which all the great religions of humankind speak."[10]

What a Journal Does

Reading journals of noted contemporaries will show that devoted journal keepers use them for a variety of purposes. Douglas Steere kept a journal from the 1930s to the 1980s in connection with his worldwide ministry among Quakers.[11] His journals report in detail meetings with people from whom he drew "wisdom in human hide." The journals interpret what he experienced. They obviously served as a firsthand source for reports to the American Friends Service Committee or Friends World Committee for Consultation and travel letters, which these groups circulated among Quakers and other friends throughout the world. Douglas's journal for the years just after World War II helped him put together an argument for the American Friends Service Committee to back a relief program for war-torn Finland.

---

10 Morton T. Kelsey, *Adventure Inward: Christian Growth through Personal Journal Writing* (Minneapolis, Minn.: Augsburg, 1980), 27.

11 See E. Glenn Hinson, *Love at the Heart of Things: A Biography of Douglas V. Steere* (Wallingford, Pa.: Pendle Hill Publications; Nashville, Tenn: Upper Room Books, 1998) regarding what Douglas called his "*Autobiography*." This unpublished work is more in the nature of a journal with no chapter divisions. For it Douglas drew from other unpublished journals and travel letters.

Thomas Merton's journals, like those of many other literary figures, were written with publication in mind.[12] Prior to entering the Abbey of Gethsemani in 1941, Merton used his journal to hone his writing skills. After entering the Trappist monastery and undertaking an earnest religious search, however, he recorded far more searching entries with his engagement with God uppermost in mind. Although in the early years he manifested some of a new convert's tendency to meet official expectations, he sought to strip off all masks and bare his soul to God. The reader can see an evolution in the journaling. Early on, Merton focused on his healing and restoration as he tried to clang monastery doors behind him and shut the world out. In the last years of his short life, he had undergone sufficient restoration to enable him to engage the world and speak to its ills as a part of his encounter with God.

Despite Douglas Steere's or Thomas Merton's published journals, the journal is a very private document, usually intended only for the eyes of the author. You do not make deeply personal entries intending or expecting the world to see them. In a journal you may record momentous experiences, thoughts or feelings, ideas, dreams, or prayers too intimate to share with any other person. You may give free rein to your imagination or release your deepest emotion. You may air your feelings and use the journal as a therapeutic tool. You may work through difficult decisions. Putting them down on paper may deepen the process of reflection.

Journals will render their greatest service as an

---

12 The Merton *Journals* have been published in seven volumes by HarperSanFrancisco: *Run to the Mountain: The Story of a Vocation* (1995); *Entering the Silence: Becoming a Monk and Writer* (1996); *A Search for Solitude: Pursuing the Monk's True Life* (1997); *Turning toward the World: the Pivotal Years* (1996); *Dancing in the Water of Life: Seeking Peace in the Hermitage* (1997); *Learning to Love: Exploring Solitude and Freedom* (1997); *The Other Side of the Mountain: The End of the Journey* (1998).

inventory of spiritual progress. Spiritual growth, just like physical growth, is slow. You may experience occasional spurts when you move from one plateau to another, but such spurts happen infrequently. In the short run, you will probably not notice your growth when it occurs an inch or so at a time. If you have not kept some kind of record, you will have no way to measure whether you have progressed at all. Journals allow you to look back over the long trajectory where you can discern improvement in your outlook on life, your relationship with God and with other people, your attitudes and responses to frustrations you encounter, your self-understanding and confidence, and, in brief, your humanity. Journal keeping will not necessarily lead to an encounter with God, but it can certainly help in the quest and improve your relationship. Inner growth can benefit immensely from keeping a journal.

What to Journal In

Some journal keepers advise buying a nicely bound diary that you would be likely to preserve and treasure, and there is still something to be said for that. A journal should have permanence. It is a sacred record. The more valuable the copybook, the more likely you are to keep up the recording and the relationship with God.

Others are less concerned about the aesthetic aspect of the journal. Douglas Steere bought bound exercise books with lined paper and often, in his characteristic concern for precision, made entries on top of entries. His major concern was to assure completeness. Thomas Merton typed his entries on loose-leaf paper and kept them in three-ring binders. Like Steere, he sometimes penned in changes and added to his entries.

In this cybernetic age many people use computers to journal. When I was still using a 1923 Underwood Standard typewriter, I was skeptical of using a computer. Would it allow for the kind of meditation that should accompany journaling? Switching to a computer has changed my mind. Composing on a computer permits me to spend time in contemplation and then revise the entries in ways scarcely allowed by either longhand or typewritten composition except by awkward scissors-and-paste methods. Using the computer, I can cut and paste with the touch of a button.

In the last analysis, the decision about your journal is very personal. You should select a copybook or method that safeguards your privacy, for you will record your innermost feelings and experiences. You have charge of everything you put in it or take out of it.

How Often to Journal

One of the first questions novices to journaling raise is whether they must do it every day. The answer may depend on the purpose served by the journal. Persons using a journal to stimulate and deepen their relationship with God will want at the outset to set aside some time each day for attentiveness to God and to themselves and to enter some reflections in the journal. Beginners in the spiritual pilgrimage, which, as Thomas Merton observes, all of us are, need to sharpen their inward eyes and ears to the Eternal transecting time. Hardly anything will assist that better than a daily discipline of writing down what has passed through mind and heart.

Now I can hear voices of protest coming from some Protestant, especially Free Church, readers: "But why must I write things down? Why can't I just rely on the Spirit? Doesn't that detract from the working of grace in my life?" In this protest are echoes of similar reactions against writing of sermons and prayers: "We must do nothing to impede full reliance on the

Holy Spirit." John Smyth, one of the first Baptists, insisted even on translation of Greek and Hebrew texts from the pulpit so that the Spirit might be fully at work in inspiration. From what I have observed in most pulpits, if rigidly adhered to, that custom might eliminate scripture readings altogether! On the contrary, writing deepens the reflection process. Elementary school teachers require students to write essays because it requires them to take greater care with their speech. Similarly, sermons, prayers, and your sorting out of thoughts and feelings all reach deeper levels when written down and impact your relationship with God more forcefully. Far from getting in the way of the Spirit, writing gives the Spirit more of a chance to work.

Having argued so insistently for a discipline of daily journaling for cultivating the inner life, I must confess that I know of no spiritual master who journaled every day, not even John Wesley or Thomas Merton, both of whom left extensive journals. Noteworthy experiences may not happen every day, and a journal can provide a good inventory of inner growth or record of inner and outer life without a daily entry. Not recording something every day, of course, should not dampen attentiveness and responsiveness to God in each day's activities and thoughts. What is important is the quality of the entries you make, whether they reflect something serious going on in the relationship with God.

Beginning with a Spiritual Autobiography

Many journalers begin with their spiritual autobiography up to the time they start journaling. The autobiography obviously will not have the detail of a journal, but it can give useful perspective, a general inventory. The object is not to tell everything that has happened in your life but to highlight experiences that would help you and others understand how you reached your present spiritual state. What are the significant moments, happenings, persons, or experiences that account for who you are? Interpret your pilgrimage. If you can, posit a theme. Perhaps a brief account of the early part of my own spiritual journey can offer some guidance.

I would entitle my account "A Miracle of Grace," for little in my early years seems to give much grounds for understanding who I am today. *Grace, phase one.* I was born into a family of conflict. My father was an alcoholic, and my earliest memories of anything are of my mother and father fighting, physically and verbally. My early vocabulary would have embarrassed sailors.

Religiously, my life did not look promising, either. My first memories of church are of attending seances. At the time my mother belonged to a spiritualist church. Spiritualists believe the soul of the deceased remains in the vicinity of the earth three years after death. During that time, the bereaved can communicate with the souls of the dead through a medium. My mother, although a Baptist, turned in that direction to seek answers to a failing marriage and other crises. When my father was sober, he was an atheist; when he was drunk, he was a fundamentalist. When drunk, he took us to revival meetings at the Cave Spring Landmark Missionary Baptist Church. He loved to sing and had a fine baritone voice. Sometimes he could barely stand, but he was one of few in that church who could carry a tune.

Not much there offered any promise in the religious search in which I have spent my life unless it was perplexity. But at the same time scratching around in the soil of my soul were some ordinary saints. Fleta and Osse Marsh, my aunt and uncle, were among them. They were not pushy about faith, but they lived it. When my mother and father divorced, they took my older brother and reared him. A short time later, they took two cousins and cared for them when their mother had to enter a tuberculosis sanitorium for four years. Bertha Brown, my teacher most of my eight years in a one-room country school, was another. When my whole world was falling apart with my parents' divorce, she would put her hand on my shoulder and say, "You can make it, Glenn. You can make it." And I knew I could because she always did. She was so faithful. In all those years she missed only one half day of school. That was the day it snowed fourteen inches, and the temperature dropped to twenty-three degrees below zero. But she got there at noontime. None of her pupils got there, but we knew she had because the stove was warm the next morning. The fire would have gone out completely had she not gotten there. G. C. Busch, owner of the general store five miles from our farm, was a fourth ordinary saint. When we needed food for our table or feed for our cattle, a G. C. Busch and Sons' truck always came, and his sons always told my mother the same thing. "It's all right if you can't pay now, Mrs. Hinson, Dad won't mind." I don't know how many were not able to repay him at all during those depression years, but my mother always tried. When my mother could no longer pay the six dollars a month rent on the eighty-acre farm we lived on, we moved to a farm owned by G. C. Busch, rent free. He reminds me of the "Inasmuchers" of Jesus' parable of kingdom character in Matthew 25:31-46. He was downright good.

Grace, phase two. I made a profession of faith in a Baptist church at age eleven or twelve one summer when I worked on a farm at Cuba, Missouri, which adjoined my uncle and aunt's farm. When I returned home, however, I did not have much encouragement to sustain the zeal of my commitment until I moved to St. Louis to work and to attend Washington University. Living there with my aunt and uncle, who had moved from Cuba to St. Louis by that time, I found their example of church attendance and participation compelling.

Going to Washington University, however, I soon found myself in a crisis of both faith and vocation.

The vocational crisis had to do with the wrong reasons for the choice I had made. I had gone to Washington University to study law and would have entered law school in my fourth year. I chose that vocation because I thought it assured prestige and money. Having grown up in poverty in the Missouri Ozark Mountains, I coveted most those two things. At that excellent school, though, professors kept asking, "What are you going to do with your education, with your life, besides serve yourself?" By the end of my second year, worn down from working about thirty-five hours a week while carrying a full course load, I found myself in a deep crisis about my vocation.

Meantime, I was plunged into a crisis of faith. Professors demanded, "How do you know what you believe? How do you prove it?" Unfortunately, the pastor of the church I attended was a fundamentalist. When I took questions to him, he would say, "If you believe that, you will go straight to hell." I, for understandable reasons, did not take many questions to him. Doubts began to overwhelm me. Early in my third year, I began lying awake at night pondering vocation and faith. One night, after a fitful slumber I awakened at 2:00 A.M., sat bolt upright in bed, and John 8:32 was burning on my mind, "You will know the truth, and the truth will make you free." All of a sudden, it rolled over me, "If God is truth, if Christ is truth, then nothing you discover by any legitimate means of inquiry can change that. The truth that matters is personal, and only you can answer whether you will live life from the vantage point of a relationship with God or not." I was free indeed!

A short time afterward, the vocational decision resolved itself. During a revival meeting, a young South African minister showed a film on missions. The film spoke to me with a clear voice: "There *is* something you can do with your life besides serve yourself. You can serve God by ministering to others."

I could tell the rest of my story, but this part will supply enough of a frame for you to do the same. The overarching theme of my story has been articulated well in that universally favorite hymn "Amazing Grace." "'Tis grace hath brought me safe thus far, and grace will lead me home."

The Journaling Process

Developing the discipline of journaling may require you to make a convincing case for it. Introverts will probably find it easier than extroverts. If you are having trouble journaling, write down some of the values you will obtain. (1) It will give me information about myself that I can go back to in later years. (2) It will be pleasant to recall especially significant experiences. (3) It will stimulate inner creativity. (4) It will cultivate my imagination. (5) It will help me work out some issues with which I am struggling. (6) It will permit me to air some feelings I dare not talk about to other people. (7) I need a discipline in my spiritual life.

How much time you spend will vary, but it is a good practice at first to set aside the same period each day. Human beings depend very much on habit to get the most out of what they are doing. Any time of day will be fine, but it should not be simply tacked on when you are not really functional. Remember that this is a time of attentiveness to God about what is going on in your life.

If you are to be fully attentive and transparent, you will want to find a quiet *place* where you are not likely to be interrupted, whether by persons, telephones, or loud noises. Journaling is a mini-retreat. You draw back from the press and struggle of the day to engage God in conversation about what has been happening. You go apart momentarily not as a flight *from* the world but to become collected again and thus to return better prepared to meet its needs.

Becoming collected will require the *laying aside of preoccupations and distractions.* You may come to these quiet times laden with a lot of baggage—troubling thoughts, conversations, work to be done, letters to be written. How do you get these out of mind and heart long enough to engage God about yourself? Before Morton Kelsey begins a journaling session, he writes down on scraps of paper all of the things that are crowding his mind and tosses them into a box so that he won't worry about forgetting them. He comes back to them after he has completed his journaling. Others rely more on some form of meditation exercise to relax and become attentive.

A variety of *exercises ranging from Yoga to Zen will help you relax and prepare* for the central concern of conversation with God. A very simple method that many have found useful is to think relaxation of each part of your body for a few seconds beginning with the big toe on the right foot and going part by part to the top of the head. It takes about ten minutes and, if you maintain concentration, results in real relaxation. The simpler the exercise, the better. The goal is an inward quiet wherein you can hear "the still, small voice" of God as in other forms of prayer.

Journaling of the type being considered here is *a type of prayer.* It is conversation, communication, communion with God written down. As in oral prayer, you will not have trouble articulating concerns, making requests, entreating, and informing God about your situation. However, because of your cultural conditioning, you will struggle to be honest, candid, and transparent with God, especially on paper. Here you will need again to learn from the psalmists. If you are going to deepen your relationship with God, you must be utterly open and unmasked. As Thomas Merton has expressed it, you must strip away your false self and get down to your true self. God can accept you just as you are with all your faults and blemishes and transform you into the person you really can become. Openness can be facilitated by remembering that you are infinitely loved of God, a heavenly Parent who goes out both to receive the prodigal as a son and to encourage the pouty elder brother who refused to celebrate the return of his brother (Luke 15:11-32). Before such a Loving One, you can speak with utter candor and express any concern. Writing it down may clarify and mature your deeper longings.

Conversation, though, has another side at which you may not be so apt, namely, listening. No matter how devout, you should always be reticent to make claims about hearing God, of course. You should be modest enough to admit uncertainty in your interpretation of God's directives. At the same time you can recognize with the saints of all the ages, as pointed out in chapter 3, that God "speaks" through nature, history, your life, and sometimes more or less directly in dreams or visions. In journaling you are engaging in an intensive process of reflection and recording what you are "hearing" and "seeing."

Excerpts from a Personal Journal

Recognizing that you may catch on more readily from examples, I will share some excerpts from a journal that I kept almost daily during a period of sabbatical study at the Ecumenical Institute for Advanced Studies, Tantur, near Jerusalem in Israel, in the spring of 1976. On April 4 I recorded my reactions to the absence of certain friends from the Sunday worship service that I led.

The curious and, I have to admit though I am embarrassed to do so, disturbing thing was the absence of several who showed up at luncheon— . . . [I proceeded to list names and conjecture why different people were not present].

Now—my feelings. It is strange how fragile one's ego is on such a thing. I thought my ego-strength would avoid feelings like that, but that is a fickle thing. I have no desire to be in the limelight, but if things don't turn out well when I am, I am crushed. I suppose my feelings can be evaluated positively in the sense that I take everybody seriously. Should I? It's hard to say.[13]

After a visit to Yad Vashem (the Holocaust Memorial) in Jerusalem on April 6:

God—how many death camps the Nazis had. One building has the ashes of many victims. The other is a museum which tells the story from Hitler's rise to power in 1933 to the founding of Israel in 1948. The pictures starkly remind one of [humanity's] capacity for bestiality. Incredible! Incredible! Incredible! Experiments with human guinea pigs. Starvation of masses. Tortures. Execution of children, the old, the weak. Mass graves. Working people until they dropped dead. Lampshades of human skin. Soap of human fat. Mockery. Ridicule.

What kind of warped, demon-possessed mind could have invented the solution to the "Jewish question" (Judenfrage)? How could a whole nation swallow such a "solution"? How could they vote to consolidate all power under the Fuhrer in 1934? Was it just a "big lie" so well told? Or was it a pragmatism which is willing to accept any solution which brings economic benefits? Show us, O Fuhrer, the way to go and we will follow you like a dog!

Still—no one can imagine, apart from that context, how human feeling, how the love which belongs to us by nature, could be so suppressed that this systematic

---

13 E. Glenn Hinson, *Unpublished Journal,* Jerusalem, Israel, spring 1976, 8-9.

extermination could occur. Say it didn't happen, Lord! Say it didn't happen! Yet the evidence is all there.[14]

Palm Sunday, April 11, on a walk from Bethany into the city of Jerusalem:

> Now we go to Bethany to retrace the steps of Jesus! As many times as I've read Egeria, I can't figure out whether I could have similar excitement or not. If I had come by the arduous means by which she came, I probably would. Travel is too easy in our technological age for us to appreciate *places* so much—even *Holy* places.[15]

An April 19, 1:30 A.M. entry recorded some complaints:

> The shape of the Tantur show has become clear to me little by little. It is chiefly a Lutheran-Catholic affair. [I reviewed the activities of the semester to illustrate the point.]
>
> The experience here has been a negative one for me from an ecumenical viewpoint. Several Lutherans won't take communion with anyone except Lutherans. The monks won't take it with anyone except Roman Catholics. The latter did offer it to everyone at the Easter vigil after they had "baptized" all of us. Normally I accept every invitation but not this one. If the monks can offer communion this time, why not otherwise unless now we are *properly* baptized into the one great, true Church? Something is rotten in Denmark, and Tantur.
>
> My voice has bothered me a lot here. The notorious chilly wind seems to be the chief cause, but I'm probably

---

14 Ibid., 10-11.
15 Ibid., 12-13.

also feeling frustrated and angry. I do wish I could handle such feelings better. When I speak, I have to "warm up" a while to get my voice freed up. It's so embarrassing when I muff up as I did on the prayer this morning. But I couldn't do any better. Perhaps I should stop trying to sing too. That doesn't help.[16]

April 24 on a trip to Hebron and Mamre:

Hebron is located in the Valley of Eshkol where the spies, Joshua, Caleb, et al., found huge clusters of grapes. One must imagine grapes all over the area when the spies came even as today. We saw no giants, however.[17]

May 3 in Jerusalem:

Today I waited for the children at school. A little girl came by as I sat on the balustrade along the porch. Here was my instant reflection:
Impish-faced six-year-old,
Nose freckled and turned up,
Taking everything in—
Oh, how beautiful the age of innocence.[18]

Journaling Dreams

Many journalers record dreams. According to Carl Jung, dreams are a key to the subconscious, the very large part of the human psyche that is not dependent on the physical senses. At

---

16 Ibid., 16, 18-19.
17 Ibid., 25-26.
18 Ibid., 30.

the level of the subconscious, human beings have powerful experiences that impact them deeply. If properly interpreted, dreams can help people understand themselves and make important decisions about their lives. Although I have not relied significantly on dreams to obtain personal guidance and must confess some fear that heavy reliance on them has often led people astray, their use by the saints throughout the ages is too consistent to allow anyone to dismiss them. The Hebrew prophets, Jesus, Paul, the martyrs, and the saints received through dreams a word from God. Records of life-shaping dreams turn up often in journals. The young noblewoman Perpetua, for instance, reported that she had found reassurance in dreams that her brother, who had died at age seven, no longer suffered from the disease that claimed his life and that she would have the ability to face death in the arena with "manly" courage.[19] John Bunyan evidently dreamed *The Pilgrim's Progress*. It came to him, he reported in his apology for it, "like sparks that from the coals do fly,"[20] and he presented it under the guise of a dream. John Woolman noted in his *Journal* several dreams that strengthened his witness against slavery, war, and other injustices. He relied heavily on them.[21] Dorothy Steere recorded in her "Reminiscences" two dreams that helped her to accept herself as a person in her own right independent of her distinguished husband, Douglas.[22]

How will journaling assist in dealing with dreams? In much the same way it fosters spiritual growth. By writing a dream down, you have a record of it to which you can return. In the case of dreams or visions the record is important because the meaning seldom becomes immediately clear. If on first asking

---

19 *The Martyrdom of Saints Perpetua and Felicita*, 3-4, 7-8, 10.
20 John Bunyan, *The Pilgrim's Progress*, ed. James Blanton Wharey, 2d ed. (Oxford: Clarendon Press, 1960, 1967).
21 See John Woolman, *Journal*, ed. Moulton, 161-62, 191-92.
22 Dorothy M. Steere, *"Reminiscences."*

what the dream means you do not get an interpretation, you can wait a while and go back to it. If you have trouble interpreting, you can take what you have recorded in your journal to someone with expertise in interpreting dreams. Dreams are almost always symbolic and may require an expert to unravel their nuances. When you have arrived at an interpretation that seems meaningful, you can record it in your journal too.

Deepening the Engagement with God at the Heart of the World

In the last analysis, the goal of journaling is to deepen your engagement with God at the heart of the world. If, as Teilhard de Chardin posits in one of his prayers, you do not lift even a little finger without some thought, at least infinitesimally, of contributing to something definitive, that is to say, to God's work, then you should feel free to bring every thought, feeling, person, place, or event in life into this conversation with God. Reflecting on these at a deeper level required for recording something about them will force you to greater personal depths.

Some dangers are involved in this process. Journaling, like writing your spiritual autobiography, may cause you to dredge up some buried painful memories that kept you from moving forward and upward. For anyone who is willing to count the cost, however, it is a price well worth paying.

Chapter 5

MAKING THE MOST OF YOUR TIME

Effective leadership of any kind is closely tied to proper use of time. Yet time seems to be a problem in modern American culture, but in contradictory ways. On one side, some do not know what to do with the time that they have. They have too much time. Time hangs heavy. They suffer boredom as the minutes, hours, days, and weeks slip by. On the other side, some do not have enough time. There aren't enough hours in the day to do all they want to do. The hours, days, weeks, and years are too short. They go without sleep or rest or even food in order to get more accomplished. They race frantically through crowded calendars.

The contradictory nature of the time conundrum shows that the problem is not with time itself, however much scholars may philosophize about it, but with your *use* of time. In the Christian view time is a gift, a precious gift, and you have to be the best steward of time that you can. In the New Testament you will find two Greek words translated as time: *chronos* and *kairos*. *Chronos*, from which we get chronology, chronometer, and other English words, refers to measured time—the ticktock of the clock, the rhythm of the metronome, the calendar. *Kairos* is purposeful time, time filled with meaning. As Oscar Cullmann has pointed out in his classic *Christ and Time*,[1] the coming of God in Jesus Christ has raised time to a new level, caused time to take on new significance. In a Lukan perspective God has come, as it were, "in the midst of time"[2] in order to redeem it, and you take part in that redemptive process. You must not waste time, kill time, or use time for malignant and destructive purposes. You want, rather, to turn *chronos* into *kairos*.

How will you make the most of your time? The solution that scriptures suggest does not begin with some kind of time management, arranging and rearranging crowded calendars or making suggestions on how to spend idle hours. Those changes will doubtless occur if you do the best with the time you have. But to begin with a schedule is to treat symptoms rather than the disease itself. The correct order would appear to be the one Jesus suggested in Matthew 6:33: "Seek first God's mysterious Presence and God's okaying of you, and all these other things will fall into place" (AP).

The Symptoms

How to use time is not a new problem for Christians. The Apostle Paul cautioned the Colossians about time and urged them to make "the most of the time [*kairos*]" (Col. 4:5). In their case he was concerned about observance of customs such as Sabbaths, new moons, festivals, and fasts or pursuit of "the elemental spirits [*stoicheia*] of the universe" (2:8), which were canceled or negated by the coming of God in Christ. The first

---

[1] Oscar Cullmann, *Christ and Time: The PrimitiveChristian Conception of Time and History*, trans. Floyd V. Filson (Philadelphia: Westminster Press, 1950).

[2] This phrase was coined by Hans Conzelmann, *Die Mitte der Zeit: Studien zur Theologie des Lukas* (Tubingen: J. C .B. Mohr [Paul Siebeck], 1954).

Christians had considerable trouble sorting out their relationship to both Jewish and Gentile customs. Too often, they squandered time on fruitless endeavors.

In a more secular age such as ours, you will not make the most of time in other ways. One is by *nonuse*. For a Christian leader this will rarely mean deliberate wasting of time, although that is a common problem in American culture. Nonuse of time will result more often from unemployment or underemployment. When I began working on this chapter, the Teamsters Union were conducting a strike against United Parcel Service, the world's largest package handler, because more than 80 percent of the recently hired UPS workforce was part-time. Part-time labor is cheaper to employers, but people who work only part-time fall below the poverty line and often lack benefits such as health insurance. Firings and forced resignations from church positions also occur with great frequency and have become one of the most serious concerns of persons who devote their lives to Christian ministry. Often these displacements happen at an age when people have difficulty obtaining another position. Years of potentially high fruitfulness are wasted.

Another way in which time is lost is by *misuse*. I should hope in the case of Christian leadership that this would not mean use of time for evil or destructive purposes, but sad to say, that does occur. Recent notorious cases include major scams, embezzlement of church funds, preachers consorting with prostitutes, sexual abuse, and numerous other offenses. What I am concerned about here, however, is poor stewardship—not using time wisely.

American culture makes effective use of an understanding of human psychology to persuade you how to use your time. Airlines feature full color pictures of blue and sunny skies, paradisal beaches, handsome and happy people, and luxurious hotels to convince you that you need to "fly their friendly skies." The appeal is usually not to actual *need* but to what Thomas Merton called "artificial and contrived needs."[3] The National Basketball Association jazzes up the wide appeal of its games featuring superstars Michael Jordan, Shaquille O'Neal, and Scottie Pippin with dazzling cartoons that prove you cannot beat basketball for an exciting time. Philip Morris plasters billboards with the Marlboro Man to convince youth they need to smoke in order to be "cool." I used to be intimidated that I couldn't be a "real he-man out there in Marlboro Country." I say "used to be" because the model who played the Marlboro Man died of lung cancer. There is a poignant and grim side to that story, though. The last three or four years of his life, the Marlboro Man pleaded with Philip Morris not to use him any more as an advertisement because he was dying as a result of the company's product. But as you drive from the Richmond, Virginia (and many another) airport into the city, you will pass a giant billboard with the Marlboro Man. Philip Morris owns the Marlboro Man's image, and he is still the company's most effective advertisement.

In such a culture all will struggle to be good stewards of their time. I love to watch basketball. During the basketball season, which has now become nearly year-round, I am fanatic about basketball—going to games, watching games on television, reading about players or anything bearing on basketball in newspapers or magazines, arguing with others about rankings, and otherwise turning basketball into a consuming passion. You can find out how high basketball stands in my estimation by stepping in front of my television during an important play. And there are people who act out such feelings in connection with their sports addiction—verbally and sometimes physically abusing opposing players and coaches, referees, other fans, and officials. Sports events have resulted in

---

3 Thomas Merton, *Faith and Violence: Christian Teaching and Christian Practice* (Notre Dame, Ind.: University of Notre Dame Press, 1968), 216.

riots. Something of proximate significance becomes an ultimate. I do not mean to suggest that you should give up re-creation, the original meaning of which I would emphasize. You do need leisure time in which you can become collected and be present where you are.[4] You do need to "waste time for God" and for yourself. My wife paints. She is a skilled oil painter. Oil painting takes much time because oils dry slowly. Consequently, Martha has often felt guilty. "Shouldn't I be doing something for the children? Shouldn't I be volunteering for something at church or at school?" I have had to explain to her that she needs this for her re-creation or, negatively put, that we could not stand to live with her if she did not do this.

A third way in which time loses its true significance is through *overuse*. This may well be the most serious problem for a Christian leader. You may crowd too much into your calendar, and your busyness squeezes the meaning out of much that you are doing. Your hurriedness prevents you from being really present to persons who seek your counsel. Quantity pushes quality ever downward.

Wayne E. Oates wrote a book entitled *Confessions of a Workaholic*.[5] In it he confessed that he did not know he was a workaholic until his wife and sons started telephoning to make appointments to see him. Some do not know about their workaholism until they have heart attacks or nervous breakdowns, their children have trouble in school or go to juvenile court, or the spouse says, "I want a divorce."

Workaholism creeps up on you, Oates observed. You can discern stages of growth. At first you go to work early and stay late. Then you look around and compare how much you are

---

[4] Douglas V. Steere pointed to this urgent need in an unpublished sermon entitled "Collected and Uncollected Man" and in a Pendle Hill Pamphlet entitled *On Being Present Where You Are* (1967).

[5] Wayne E. Oates, *Confessions of a Workaholic* (New York: World Publishing, 1971).

doing with how much everyone else is doing and pride yourself on the fact that you are doing more than anyone else. Finally, you get to the point that you cannot say no.

Professor Oates pointed out how difficult it is to deal with workaholism in our society. It is harder to confront than alcoholism or drug addiction, for they are *not* socially approved. Work is socially approved. Our industrious Puritan forebears injected the work ethic deeply into the American subconscious. "Oh, she is a real go-getter," you may hear someone say. "Why she works twenty-four hours a day, seven days a week!" That is spoken not in disparagement but in admiration. Here is a person killing herself and we applaud. We admire that. I do not believe that this admiration demonstrates a healthy attitude toward God or humanity.

The Source

Nonuse, misuse, and overuse are only symptoms. The source of the problem lies much deeper.

You may blame modern technological society for the problem you are having with your use of time. Technology receives, and often deserves, criticism for many of the disturbing aspects of modern civilization. In this case, however, if you are honest and fair, you will have to concede that technology has not taken time away from you. Technology has given you time.

Because of modern electronic technology, you can work twenty-four hours a day, seven days a week. Your grandparents usually worked from dawn to dark, for those kerosene lamps and lanterns simply did not permit long hours after dark.

Because of modern transport technology, you can travel from Washington, D.C., to London or Paris in the same amount of time it took my grandfather to drive the six miles from his farm to the nearest town with his horses and wagon.

Because of modern computer technology, you can work in minutes complicated mathematical problems that your grandparents would have spent hours solving with paper and pencil. A few years ago, I received in a box of cereal a pocket calculator that can solve fairly elaborate problems my grandfather might not have attempted.

You need not brand technology as the culprit. Technology does merely what you ask it to do—unless you have allowed yourself, as Aldous Huxley warned in *Brave New World,* to become the subject of technology. Thomas Merton panned the human plight, in *Conjectures of a Guilty Bystander,* as becoming, on one side, an "implement" or a "hand" or "a bio-physical link between machines" or, on the other side, "a mouth, a digestive system and an anus, something *through which* pass the products of his [or her] technological world, leaving a transient and meaningless sense of enjoyment."[6] If you ask what underlies this curious development, you will have to look at the dependence of your ego on affirmation through activity.

I am not suggesting here that work, meaningful activity, is unimportant to how you feel about yourself. Work is *very important* to self-esteem. No one has a lower self-image than long-term unemployed or perhaps even newly unemployed persons. In virtually every American city you will find families that have experienced unemployment for two or three generations and, as a consequence, have minimal self-esteem. Whatever the vocation, lack of meaningful activity tramples on the ego and crushes feelings of self-worth.

However, not just activity but *quantity* of activity has come to determine how people feel about themselves. Ask many people, "How are you?" and if they respond with more than a perfunctory "Okay!" ninety-nine times out of a hundred, you will hear a litany of activities. "Oh, I am so busy. I am working

---

6 Thomas Merton, *Conjectures of a Guilty Bystander* (Garden City, N.Y.: Doubleday & Co., 1966), 64.

two jobs, one forty hours a week and the other fifteen. I am involved in three different community organizations and am president of one of them. I am on seven committees at church." By the time you hear the full list you feel tired.

Have you noticed what clergy do when they get together? They pull out their appointment books and compare busyness. A game of clerical one-upsmanship gets under way. When I glance out of the corner of my left eye at a colleague's schedule and see that she has three more engagements this month than I have, I slink down into my chair in quiet humiliation. "She is needed more than I am." Or when I glance out of the corner of my right eye at another colleague's book and see that I have two more engagements, I recover some of my self-esteem. Ego! Quantity strokes self-esteem.

The Solution

If the source of the problem resides in your ego and not in anything external to you, does not Matthew 6:33 present the real solution? First, seek the God who loves with an infinite love. Let that love strengthen and shape your inner self. Then other things will begin to fall into place.

Seek First God's Mysterious Presence (the Kingdom).

If you fault the culture for your problem with time, should you not do so precisely at this point? It diverts you from the one thing that is needed for life or, better, the One who is needful for life. As Thomas Merton has remarked, Western civilization no longer has in it a place to seek Wisdom for its own sake, the Ground of Being, God[7]. Medieval monks might have elevated the contemplative life too highly above the active life, but our age and culture have surely gone to the opposite extreme in sanctifying activity for activity's sake. In the story of Mary and Martha (Luke 10:38-42) Jesus did not censure Martha's work, her ministry. Rather, he faulted her failure in her busyness to make the most of the present moment. Mary, the account says, "sat at the Lord's feet" and listened to what he was saying. But Martha was busying herself with a lot of ministry *(diakonia)*. You can readily understand and may sympathize with the exasperation Martha felt as she saw her sister. "She [Martha] stopped and said, 'Sir, doesn't it bother you that my sister sits there on her can and leaves me to do all the work? Tell her to get up and help me'"(Luke 10:40, AP). Precisely how you may feel when you see people sitting around while you work! Or in the case of many Protestants, when they think of people claiming to devote themselves to prayer rather than "doing something." Tilden Edwards told about a Washington, D.C., private school whose students liked it when one teacher introduced classes with ten minutes of silence. It was the only time in the day when they did not have to do something. But their parents objected. They were paying for that time, and they wanted their children to be "doing something" then.

Jesus' response zeroes in on the central issue for both Martha and Mary and for you. "Martha, Martha, you are worrying and are upset about a lot of things, but there is need of one. For Mary has chosen the good part which will not be taken from her" (AP). In the Greek "one" may be either neuter ("one thing") or masculine ("one person"). The one thing or, just as likely, the One who was needful was there, and Martha's busyness was keeping her from realizing that moment of grace while Mary lapped it up.

---

7 Thomas Merton, F*aith and Violence*, 217.

Henry Nelson Weiman, one of America's noted philosophers, once said, "We ought to live each moment as if all Eternity converged upon it."[8] I am not sure you can live with your wick turned up that high without burning up the wick, but you can practice what Jean-Pierre de Caussade called "the sacrament of the present moment."[9] Caussade spoke of being open to God's presence at all times and in all places. Sacrament may be defined as that through which you experience grace, God personally present. No one, surely, should have greater concern for that than a Christian leader.

Ironically, in an age when technology has multiplied the amount of things you can do in a certain amount of time, you may find life less and less meaningful precisely because you let busyness get in the way of a search for the One who is needful. You may think *doing* more and more or *acquiring* more and more will bring the ultimate happiness. Yet neither activity nor acquisition will satisfy a deeper longing or quiet the restlessness innate in human nature that Augustine spoke about in his *Confessions*. God has indeed made you for Godself, and quantity of activity only whets the appetite for more and leaves you feeling empty. It is not at all surprising that many gifted clergy, often the most dedicated, literally "burn out," consuming all the spiritual energy they have trying to satisfy every request and to please every person around them while neglecting the One who is needful.

---

[8] I owe this quotation to Huston Smith, Weiman's son-in-law, when I was Smith's student at Washington University in St. Louis.

[9] Jean-Pierre de Caussade, *The Sacrament of the Present Moment*, trans. Kitty Muggeridge (San Francisco: Harper & Row, 1989). Caussade's work has usually gone by the title *Abandonment to Divine Providence*, but the phrase "sacrament of the present moment" recurs repeatedly and is a central idea.

And God's Okaying of You.

In the Sermon on the Mount, Jesus makes it clear that achieving the character God requires far beyond human capabilities. I hope that you will bear with my paraphrase here of the text in Matthew. Whereas the ancients said, "Don't murder!" Jesus says, "Don't get angry!" (Matt. 5:21-26). Whereas the ancients said, "An eye for an eye and a tooth for a tooth!" Jesus says, "Don't retaliate! Turn the other cheek!" (5:38-42). Whereas the ancients said, "Love your neighbor and hate your enemy," Jesus says, "Love your enemies and pray for your persecutors, so that you may be children of your heavenly Parent, for that One causes the sun to rise on evil and good and the rain to pour on righteous and unrighteous" (5:43-45). Then the clincher among these impossibilities: "You shall be perfect as your heavenly Parent is perfect." In what sense "perfect"? In the context the answer is clear—"perfect in love." God wants you to love with the same unqualified, unconditional love with which God loves. The infinite love of God alone can effect such a change in you and, at the same time, accept you when, inevitably, you fail to measure up to perfection.

Matthew might have pulled together these words of Jesus as a kind of handbook for Christian missionaries to use in instructing new converts.[10] The most notable of early Christian missionaries, the Apostle Paul, would have agreed with this perspective as applied to himself. Had he not recognized it, he had strong insistence from the cranky and contentious Corinthians. He lacked the apostolic credentials of a Peter. He could not preach like an Apollos. He was not handsome and was often hard to understand. His defense rested in God's okaying:

"We have this confidence with God through Christ. Not

---

[10] See Krister Stendahl, *The School of St. Matthew and Its Use of the Old Testament* (Uppsala: G. W. K. Gleerup, 1954), 24.

that we are competent from ourselves to be considered anything as from ourselves. But our competence is from God, who has made us competent to be ministers of a new covenant, not of letter but of spirit" (2 Cor. 3:4-6, author's translation). None, surely, knew better than Paul that the task of ministry is too great and that we are too small.

Paul had an immense vision of his own task. He wanted to plant the gospel in every major center of trade and culture in the Roman Empire that it had not yet reached, to stay long enough to assure a community that could survive there, and to train leaders to continue his work. From the moment of his conversion, however, he ran into opposition—at first from those who considered his conversion suspect and then from those who steadfastly resisted the inclusion of Gentiles without their meeting all requirements for entrance into the Jewish community. The opposition often grew nasty. He described himself in his "harsh" letter to the Corinthians as "afflicted in every way but not hemmed in, perplexed but not despairing, persecuted but not giving up, knocked down but not destroyed, always bearing in my body the death of Christ in order that the life of Jesus may be evident in our body" (2 Cor. 4:8-10, author's translation).

Paul was well aware of life's vulnerabilities. He spoke about a "thorn in the flesh," which he had "urged the Lord three times to take it away from me" (2 Cor. 12:8, author's translation). No one can say for sure what Paul's "thorn in the flesh" was. Some evidence in the Corinthian letters indicates that he suffered from eye trouble, which disfigured his face. There are also hints of epilepsy, and that in a day before there were medications to control epileptic seizures. Although we cannot be certain what the problem was, we can be sure that Paul had an intense desire to be rid of it. He wrote, "I urged [almost *commanded* because of the verb's intensity] the Lord three times to take it away from me." "Three times" in Hebrew idiom would not mean "I prayed on three separate occasions and let it go at that." No, it means: I pulled out all the stops.

Paul did not get the answer he wanted, but he received one that supplied the axle around which his theology would turn: "My grace is sufficient for you, for my power is perfected in weakness" (2 Cor. 12:9). Grace here must mean more than the popular Protestant definition, "God's unmerited favor." It means, rather, God's gift of Godself, God's presence in the risen Christ, in the Spirit. The Christian life is life in Christ, life in the Spirit. "In Christ" the Christian is able to cope with whatever life brings. "I have strength for all occasions in the one who empowers me" (Phil. 4:13), Paul reminded the Philippians during the worst days of his imprisonment.

The reason for that can be found in the second part of this word of revelation, "for my power is perfected in weakness." God's power, love power, works in human vulnerability. That perspective is one that many in our age and culture have difficulty understanding. We know a lot about power. Some say that our culture is obsessed with power. We want more power to run bigger electric generators so that we can have more comforts and conveniences or more power to put up bigger payloads into space to terrify our enemies so they will not dare to threaten us. But our power logic, Paul would point out, is not God's power logic. Our power logic runs, "The weak are weak. The strong are strong. In weakness is weakness. In strength is strength." God's power logic runs, "In your human weakness you may find my power." That is the logic of the Suffering God, which we see throughout history. That is the logic of the Cross, the core of Paul's theology. He was not ashamed of the gospel, "for it is the power of God to salvation" (Rom. 1:16).

In the final analysis, Paul would say, Christian ministry, indeed Christian life, depends on learning how to let down like a swimmer letting down into the water to discover the buoyancy that holds up the body. Through the centuries the saints have discovered that truth again and again. We live in a sea of love, they said. We are surrounded by love. And if we will let ourselves down to discover the love that is at the heart of things, we can face the fearful unknown. Isn't that what the psalmist knew centuries ago?

> Even though I walk through the darkest valley,
>   I fear no evil;
> for you are with me;
>   your rod and your staff—
>   they comfort me. (Ps. 23:4)

Paul discerned in his experience God's strange logic: "We have this treasure [the gospel] in clay pots in order that the thrust of power may be God's and not from us" (2 Cor. 4:7, author's translation). Typical human logic would cause us more often than not to opt for the powerful. We would have chosen the Egyptians, the Babylonians, the Assyrians, the Persians to carry out a world mission, not the motley nomadic tribes who followed Abraham. We expect the more powerful to carry out their purposes. How readily throughout history have Christians linked up with the powers that be! "But," Paul insisted, "God chose the foolish things of the world to shame the wise, and . . . the weak things of the world to shame the strong, and . . . the ignoble and contemptible things, the nothings, to nullify the somethings, so that no one may boast before God" (1 Cor. 1:27-29).

What is the logic of God in choosing the common and ordinary to do God's work in the world? A human being will probably never comprehend it, but Paul tried. If God had chosen the extraordinary, you would think that you had within yourself what it takes. By choosing the ordinary "clay pots" rather than gold, silver, or finely ornamented glassware you would have found in houses of Paul's day, God left no mistake. You are not and you do not have in yourself the transcendent power that works in your weakness! Thanks be to God! The wise first step in ministry, therefore, is to seek God and God's okaying of you with the power perfected in weakness.

The Other Things Will Fall into Place.

To arrange priorities, then, you must begin at the center where, as Thomas Kelly has said so beautifully, "the breath and stillness of Eternity are upon us."[11] Around that center your priorities begin to appear in their proper order. Now this is not to say that the whole time problem will disappear as if by magic when you begin there. You will always struggle to "have a sense of things that really matter" (Phil. 1:10), but the growth of God's love in understanding and every sensitivity in the inner person will give you the motive and ability to keep assessing and revising your use of time. Because each person's situation is unique, it is best to think of priorities.

Your first priority should be *some focused time for communion, communication, or conversation with God.* Ideally, you will want to be attentive to God in everything you are doing—to pray without ceasing. Practically, however, in an environment constantly vying for attention, you need some time deliberately set apart for God, the mini-retreats I wrote of earlier. It is very easy, especially for someone involved in Christian leadership, to make excuses here. "Well, God, you understand. I'm involved in your business. I don't have time now to stop and talk or to listen." What you are really saying here is, "I don't have time for self-care." All too many clergy put the question

---

[11] Thomas R. Kelly, *A Testament of Devotion* (New York: Harper Brothers. 1941) 74.

the wrong way, asking, "Can I afford the time this would take?" The proper question is, "Can I afford *not* to take this time?" Ministry without "Sabbath time" focused on God will soon dry up all of your personal energies for ministry. Self-care of this sort must head the priority list.

Next in order of priorities are *persons*. Among these, the people who are closest must come first—spouse, children, and other family members. The author of the code for clergy in 1 Timothy 3 raised a sound query about this: "If anyone does not know how to stand at the head of his own household, how will that person care for the church of God?" How easy it is for a clergyperson to "marry" the job and to make excuses to intimate family. "You understand. I'm involved in the Lord's work, and I'm so busy." Spouse and children do not understand. The divorce rate among clergy is similar to the divorce rate among the population in general. And there has long been awareness of the special problems of "preachers' kids," much of which is related to neglect or artificial expectations stemming from the position clergy hold.

Other persons—colleagues, friends, parishioners, those who belong to your extended family—would come next in an ever widening circle. Why this emphasis on persons? Because, at least in the case of most clergy, *projects* so easily override everything else. A survey conducted by Samuel W. Blizzard showed that clergy spent more than half of their time in administrative or organizational duties, a fact that may explain why certain types fare better in institutional roles in religion than other types (see appendix). Notwithstanding very different ideas about how they should spend their time, Protestant clergy allocated 18 percent to their role as preacher and priest, 5 percent as teacher, 26 percent as pastor, and 51 percent as administrator or organizer.[12]

This ordering of priorities—sparing time for God and putting persons high on the list—does not depend on *quantity* of time allocated (the largest amount for communion with God, the next largest for persons, and the smallest for projects). Although *projects* should come after giving time to God and persons, projects will doubtless claim the lion's share of any leader's time. In your prioritizing, you make the claim that you will not permit any project to crowd out time for God or for other persons. You want your relationship with God to enter into everything you are doing. As Paul urged the Colossians, "Whatever you do, in word or deed, do everything in the name of the Lord Jesus, giving thanks to God the Father through him" (Col. 3:17).

To remain open to the sacrament of the present moment and to claim the priority of God who claims you, pray with George Herbert:

> Teach me, my God and King,
> In all things thee to see,
> And what I do in anything,
> To do it as for thee.[13]

---

[12] Samuel W. Blizzard, *The Protestant Parish Minister: A Behavioral Science Interpretation*, Society for the Scientific Study of Religion Monograph Series, 5 (Storrs, Conn.: Society for the Scientific Study of Religion, 1985), 100. Blizzard completed his study in 1957 and published some aspects of it shortly afterward. See "Parish Minister's Self-Image of His Master Role," *Pastoral Psychology 9* (December 1958): 25-32; and "Parish Minister's Self-Image and Variability in Community Culture," *Pastoral Psychology 10* (October 1959): 27-36. However, illness prevented him from completing the writing of the full report before his death in 1976.

[13] George Herbert, verse from "The Elixir" in *The Temple* from *The Works of George Herbert in Prose and Verse* Vol. II, (London: Bell and Daldy, 1859), 212.

Chapter 6

MAINTAINING BALANCE

Healthy spirituality requires a balance of experiential, intellectual, social, and institutional dimensions.[1] These are like four legs under a table. Take away one leg and the table will wobble. Take away more than one and it will fall. All too often, Americans try to maintain their relationships with God by standing on one leg or, at best, to make a spiritual table with one long leg and three shorter ones, each perhaps of different lengths. Indeed, different religious groups have come into existence with the object of offsetting an imbalance by accenting just one of these emphases.

Some emphasize the *experiential* dimension almost to the exclusion of the other three. Charismatic groups have popped up throughout Christian history to redress the balance on this side. So Montanists during the second century, spiritualists during the sixteenth, and Pentecostals and charismatics in the twentieth. All have reminded their contemporaries that God, the

---

[1] Three of these dimensions—experiential, intellectual, and institutional—have been drawn from Baron Friedrich von Hügel. In practice, however, he also insisted on the social dimension.

living God, is as present and active in human life in the present day as in the age of the apostles. Faith without experience is dead.

Others, fearful of emotion and mystery, underscore the *intellectual* dimension with limited concern for experiential, social, or institutional elements. The scholastic systems of thought produced by the universities during the Middle Ages and after, wherein the head took precedence over the heart, are examples of this intellectual dimension in faith. The Enlightenment of the seventeenth century and after, however, spurred this process forward as people distressed with religious conflicts and wars substituted rational religion for revealed. Debates over the validity of religious experiences of the so-called Great Awakening split religious groups. Out of the controversy among Congregationalists came Unitarianism with its pronounced accent on reason. Unitarians contended that they would believe only what is provable by reason. Unitarians opined that the biblical revelation is not reasonable and that they would rely on empirical science and not on revelation. Curiously, Christian fundamentalism, countering this rationalism, adopted the same approach in reverse. We will accept only what we find in the Bible as empirically reliable. "The Bible says it. I believe it. That settles it," Bailey Smith, a recent president of the Southern Baptist Convention, explained. Where anything conflicts with the content of the Bible, whether scientifically, historically, philosophically, or in any other way, fundamentalists will reject the empirical data. "That's a fact" frequently punctuates fundamentalist sermons and speeches, and the statement refers to biblical content.

Others accentuate the *social* dimension to the virtual exclusion of the other three. *Social* may mean different things to different persons. For some, faith is fellowship, belonging to a family; for others, it is service and/or action, faith working through love. Only if you are with others or doing something for others can you be said to have an authentic spirituality. On the eve of World War II Thomas Kelly chided Quakers, who surpass other Christian groups in social consciousness, for letting their investment in social concerns drain away their attention to the Eternal Now and warned that this reversal of order would result in the drying up and misdirecting of social concern. Too many in the Society of Friends, he lamented, had shifted their focus to this world, time, and the temporal order and made time the judge of Eternity. He saw in this "a lamentable reversal of the true order of dependence. Time is no judge of Eternity. It is the Eternal who is the judge and tester of time."[2]

Still others, perhaps the majority, including a significant percentage of religious leaders, act as if their religious commitments and obligations are taken care of in an *institutional* manner without much thought about the other dimensions. The spiritual life has to do mainly with belonging to a particular congregation, taking part in church school, attending meetings, giving money, and sharing in social functions. Find a comfortable pew, sit back, relax, and enjoy the ride!

Each of these *dimensions* is essential to a well-rounded spirituality. A healthy relationship with God *is* experiential, intellectual, social, and institutional. Recognize and remember that the key lies in *balance*. The *experiential* dimension without an intellectual, social, or institutional element will lead to burnout, the consuming of spiritual energies in the quest for religious "highs." Following the Great Awakening, one whole area in the colony of New York was labeled "the burnt-over district" because the religious fervor of the Awakening had ended in widespread spiritual lethargy. When I taught at Wake Forest University in the early eighties, numerous students caught up in the charismatic movement confessed, "Dr. Hinson, I am

---

2 Thomas R. Kelly, *A Testament of Devotion* (New York: Harper Brothers, 1941), 91.

burned out." Sunday by Sunday, they had gone to charismatic churches seeking a higher "high." When, after a while, they no longer experienced what they sought, they felt depleted and let down. My standard prescription was to direct them toward the other dimensions of sound spirituality.

The *intellectual* dimension without an experiential, social, and institutional component will result in a spirituality without power or sensitivity. The frequently reiterated complaint of Protestant seminarians about loss of the fervor of faith is undoubtedly rooted in the headiness of academia. It is convenient for faculty to paper over the loss with the assurance that students need a more mature faith than the one they inherited from their parents or church school, that their hearts need to catch up with their heads. Unfortunately, though, many seminarians suffer such a blow that they fail to find a way to get head and heart together.

The *social* dimension without an experiential, intellectual, or institutional aspect will pull the plug out of the socket that supplies motive and direction for social service and action. During the 1960s, many progressive American churches got caught up in a fervent effort to be "the One for others" in the world, meeting the needs of the secular city as the place where God's kingdom is. Although much that they did was highly laudable, in their "worldly holiness" they frequently permitted "churchy" activities such as prayer, worship, and instruction to lapse, and when they did, their social energies also deteriorated. Many of those congregations soon discovered that they were ninety-five-pound weaklings trying to do the work of Charles Atlas.

The *institutional* dimension without an experiential, intellectual, or social dimension will fade off into a spirituality of form without vitality or wisdom or sensitivity to people. The Social Gospel movement of the late nineteenth and early twentieth centuries and the secular theology movement of the

1960s made a legitimate point when they chided Christians for retreating to "smug sanctuaries" and neglecting the world where most people live. These movements urged disciples to go *through* the world to God rather than withdraw *from* the world to God. As has been true of so many other movements, some aspects offered unhealthy extremes, but the case put by Bishop John A. T. Robinson in *Honest to God* was balanced and persuasive: "The purpose of worship is not to retire from the secular into the department of the religious, let alone to escape from 'this world' into 'the other world,' but to open oneself to the meeting of the Christ in the common, to that which has the power to penetrate its superficiality and redeem it from its alienation."[3]

The main point in all of this is *balance*. When Baron von Hügel directed his niece Gwendolyn Greene, Evelyn Underhill, or others, he constantly kept an eye on balance. If they became too caught up in seeking experience, he sent books and urged them to read more for the cultivation of understanding. If they got too enamored of spirituality as an academic pursuit, as he feared Underhill might, he dispatched them to the "ghetto," where they could see people hurting. If they became too obsessed with social endeavors, he reminded them of their institutional commitments. Although he shared the critique of the Roman Catholic Church advanced by the modernists, for whom he served as a kind of spiritual guide, he did not lose faith in the institution itself.

Finding and maintaining balance in the spiritual life, of course, is not easy, and I suspect that it is more difficult for professional religious than it is for ordinary saints. To understand how you might achieve balance, you must look more closely at each of the four dimensions.

---

3 John A. T. Robinson, *Honest to God* (London: SCM Press; Philadelphia: Westminster Press, 1963), 87.

The Experiential Dimension

Faith begins in awe, not in cognition. "When mind and soul agree," Abraham Heschel has said, "belief is born. But first our hearts must know the shudder of adoration."[4] In his characteristically poetic way he observed, "Faith is a blush in the presence of God."[5] A whole row of saints would back up this observation.

The ancient Hebrews never sought to "prove" God; they simply assumed that God is. "Fools say in their hearts, 'There is no God,'" a psalmist says (Pss. 14:1; 53:1). "You arouse the human being to take joy in praising you," Christianity's greatest Latin theologian prayed in opening his *Confessions*, "for you have made us for yourself, and our heart is restless until it rests in you."[6] The first motion of faith comes from God, Bernard of Clairvaux judged on the basis of 1 John 4:19, "We love because [God] first loved us." Bernard reassured earnest seekers with a reminder that "every soul among you that is seeking God should know that it has been anticipated by [God], and has been sought by [God] before it began to seek [God]."[7] "The heart has its reasons, of which reason knows nothing; we feel it in many things," observed Blaise Pascal, brilliant seventeenth-century mathematician and philosopher.[8] God is far beyond your comprehension either of what God is or if God is. Better then that you wager, for reason cannot decide. If you wager that God

---

[4] Abraham Joshua Heschel, *Man Is Not Alone: A Philosophy of Religion* (New York: Farrar, Straus & Giroux, 1951), 74.

[5] Ibid., 91.

[6] Augustine *Confessions* 1.1.1, in *The Confessions of St. Augustine*, trans. John K. Ryan (Garden City, N.Y.: Image Books, 1960), 43.

[7] Bernard of Clairvaux *Sermon 84 on the Song of Songs* 2; Library of Christian Classics, XIII:74-75.

[8] Blaise Pascal, *Pensées*, ed. Louis Lafuma, trans. John Warrington (London: J. M. Dent & Sons; New York: E. P. Dutton, 1960), 224.

is, and it turns out that God is not, then you have lost nothing. If you wager that God is not, and it turns out that God is, then you have lost everything. But if you wager that God is, and it turns out that God is, then you have gained everything.[9] "There is that near you which will guide you," the early Quaker saint Isaac Penington assured others and urged, "O! wait for it, and be sure ye keep to it."[10] Rufus M. Jones, distinguished Quaker philosopher, spoke of a "double search." You seek God, but just as surely God also seeks you.[11]

I am fully aware that some notable Protestant theologians such as Karl Barth and Reinhold Niebuhr have looked askance at what we call mystical experience and have hurled thunderbolts at pietism. Douglas Steere, on encountering Barth at the famous Benedictine monastery of Maria Laach in 1933, found the great Swiss theologian "very critical of prayer's excessive subjectivity." When he asked Barth why he continued to go to the monastery, Barth replied, "To refute them."[12] Like Martin Luther, Protestant critics have charged that the experiential dimension of religion has produced sometimes bizarre phenomena, caused divisions within Christian ranks, and neglected serious social obligations. Such impressions have led many Christians, especially Protestants, to block out the mystical element entirely and to place their confidence in one of the other dimensions.

The saints throughout the ages, however, would counter that all authentic faith has a mystical element.[13] Not all, to be

---

[9] Ibid., 343.

[10] Isaac Penington, *Letter to the Women Friends at Armscot*, 1678, in *Quaker Spirituality*, ed. Douglas V. Steere, Classics of Western Spirituality (New York: Paulist Press, 1984), 155.

[11] Rufus M. Jones, *The Double Search: Studies in Atonement and Prayer* (Philadelphia: J. C. Winston, 1906).

[12] Douglas V. Steere, "*Autobiography*," 158.

[13] The definition of mysticism or mystical experience is still debated. Some scholars insist on extraordinary religious experience as a condition. In his

sure, will have had a profound mystical experience that they can record in the way Bernard of Clairvaux, Julian of Norwich, Catherine of Siena, Blaise Pascal, or Dag Hammarskjöld did. Their more vivid experiences, shared in lively metaphors, can help you sort out what Douglas Steere has called "holy nudges," which you experience at one time or another.

Bernard of Clairvaux spoke of the frequent "comings" of the Word—for Bernard that meant Christ. Bernard did not know when or how the Word came or departed, but Bernard "felt" the presence. In one especially graphic passage he wrote:

> I confess, then, though I say it in my foolishness, that the Word has visited me, and has even done so very often. Yet although He has often entered into my soul, I have never at any time been aware of the precise moment of His coming. I have felt that He was present; I remember later that He has been with me; I have sometimes even had a presentiment that He would come; but I have never felt His coming or His leaving. For whence He came in entering my soul, and where He went upon leaving it, by what means He has made either entrance or departure, I confess that I do not know even to this day....[14]

projected five-volume study of *The Presence of God: A History of Western Christian Mysticism*, however, Bernard McGinn has argued that "mysticism is best seen not as some distinct or independent entity or form of religion but as an *element* in concrete religious communities and traditions. . . . The diverse forms in which the mystical element has expressed itself; the varying ways in which it has interacted with institutional, intellectual, and social forms of religious life; even the degree to which it has or has not been subject to explicit formulation—in other words, everything that constitutes mysticism as a tradition—must be taken into account as a necessary, if not a totally sufficient, aspect of any contemporary theology of mysticism." *The Growth of Mysticism: From Gregory the Great Through the 12th Century* (New York: Crossroad Herder, 1996), x.

[14] Bernard of Clairvaux *Sermon 74 on the Song of Songs* 5-6, in *Varieties of Mystic Experience* by Elmer O'Brien, S.J. (New York: Mentor-Omega Book, 1964), 105.

Catherine of Siena carried on a series of *Dialogues* that led her to confirm the profound insight of Meister Eckhart that God needs us as much as we need God. How does one explain that? The only reason she could find was what Hosea discovered with Gomer, that the Mad Lover has "fallen in love with what you have made!" Even when Catherine ran away, God went looking for her. "You clothed yourself in our humanity, and nearer than that you could not have come."[15]

Blaise Pascal summed up his extraordinary experience in 1654 with the single word Fire! A genius growing up in the day of burgeoning science, Pascal experienced a series of tragedies that created a crisis in his life, which pushed him into a serious search for God. The family squabbled over his sister's entry into the convent of Port Royal. Pascal's father died. Then Pascal discovered the illness that would claim his life at age thirty-nine. He sought certainty of God like the mathematical certainty he knew. But he did not receive that divine certainty. It came, rather, in profound mystical experience that he recorded on a scrap of paper he entitled "Memorial," which was discovered sewn into the lining of his coat when he died. The chief part read:

Year of Grace 1654
Monday 23 November, feast of St. Clement, Pope and Martyr
and others in the Martyrology.
Eve of St. Crysogonus, martyr, and others.
From about half past ten at night till about half past twelve,
Fire.
God of Abraham, God of Isaac, God of Jacob,
not of the philosophers and the learned.
Certitude, certitude; feeling, joy, peace.

---

15 Catherine of Siena, *The Dialogue*, trans. Suzanne Noffke, O.P., Classics of Western Spirituality (New York: Paulist Press, 1980), 325.

God of Jesus Christ
"My God and Thy God"
Thy God shall be my God.
The world forgot and all save God.
We lay hold of Him only through the teaching of the Gospel.[16]

In notes found on his night stand after he died and published as *Markings*, Dag Hammarskjöld, secretary general of the United Nations, reflected on the happiness of saying yes to God.

The chooser's happiness lies in his congruence with the chosen,
The peace of iron-filings, obedient to the forces of the magnetic field—
Calm is the soul that is emptied of all self,
In a restful harmony—
This happiness is here and now,
In the eternal moment of co-inherence.
A happiness within you—but not yours.[17]

I could add many other accounts. These selections remind you that experience is a basic and essential ingredient of healthy spirituality. For those who have vivid and profound experiences faith is a consequence of God's initiative and not simply human striving. God constantly invades your depths and seeks to awaken within you a sense of the presence of God. Spirituality is, above all, adoring response to an infinite God who loves you with an infinite love. It is your yes to Someone.

---

16 Blaise Pascal, *Pensées*, trans. H. F. Stewart (New York: Modern Library, n.d.), 363.

17 Dag Hammarskjöld, *Markings*, trans. Leif Sjöberg and W. H. Auden (London: Faber and Faber, 1964), 51.

The Intellectual Dimension

If faith is vital and wants to grow, however, it will not remain content with experience alone. Faith will seek understanding, *fides quaerens intellectum*. It will "hunger and thirst" to know God.

A relationship with God will not mature if it does not feed itself, if it does not spend time trying to unravel the meaning of the experience that gave rise to it in the first place. It will, as it were, "hit the books," first the scriptures and then all those other records of human encounter with God that the saints have put at your disposal, to make some sense out of your relationship with the One who surpasses all human comprehension. In his monumentally influential *Rule* Benedict of Nursia assigned a significant place for *lectio divina*, reading of scriptures and other edifying materials. Those monks had a desire for God and, as Jean Leclercq, O.S.B., has beautifully shown,[18] a love of learning precisely because growth in the inner life depends on getting to know God, and getting to know God requires applying the mind to that end.

You see this point confirmed in the levels of prayer that the saints posited in the Middle Ages. Hugo of St. Victor, a monastery just outside Paris, spoke of three grades of the knowledge of God—cogitation, meditation, and contemplation.[19] In the fourteenth century Walter Hilton gave a helpful explanation of the stages. The first consists of knowledge of God "through reason, human teaching, and the study of Holy Scripture." It is the way taken by scholars and

---

[18] Jean Leclercq, O.S.B., *The Love of Learning and the Desire for God: A Study of Monastic Culture*, trans. Catharine Misrahi (New York: Fordham University Press, 1961).

[19] Hugo of St. Victor *Nineteen Sermons on Ecclesiastes*; LCC, XIII:90-91.

lacks "spiritual savor" and "inward sweetness in God."[20] "Love on fire with devotion" is Hilton's second stage, which "consists principally in affection, without light for the understanding of spiritual things." This is the way of ordinary saints who experience "fervor of love and spiritual sweetness."[21] The third stage, "love on fire with contemplation," entails both cognition and affection, but here you are "taken out of the physical senses" and experience "a soft, sweet burning love." You can begin to experience this stage in the present life, but its fullness is reserved for the bliss of heaven.[22]

Many followed in the footsteps of Plato and Augustine in emphasizing the value of self-knowledge for knowing God. Augustine avowed in his *Soliloquies*, a dialogue between him and his Reason just after his conversion, that he wanted earnestly to know nothing but "God and the soul, that is what I desire to know."[23] God has made you "in the image of God" (Gen. 1:27). If you truly get to know your "self," you may at the same time find the "SELF," whose center, the medieval mystics thought, is everywhere and whose circumference is nowhere.

True knowledge of God will come not from cognition but from love, however. That is why the saints have resorted so readily to the analogy of marriage found in the Song of Songs. What you want to do is to fall head over heels in love with God—to "love God with all [the] heart, soul, mind, and strength" (Mark 12:30). Growth in your relationship requires getting to know God ever more intimately, just as growth in a marriage does. Infatuations may occur at first sight, but a deep, abiding, storm-weathering relationship takes a lot of searching to grasp the mystery of the other person. You must be honest to

---

[20] Walter Hilton, *The Stairway of Perfection*, trans. M. L. Del Mastro (Garden City, N.Y.: Image Books, 1979), 66-67.

[21] Ibid., 67-68.

[22] Ibid., 70-71.

[23] Augustine *Soliloquies* 1.7; NPNF, Series 1, VII:539.

admit your limitations here. No matter how bright, no matter how loving, no matter how energetic, you will never fully know God, notwithstanding God's efforts to communicate Godself to you through Israel and Jesus of Nazareth and through your experience. Nevertheless, you throw yourself into that endeavor with all the energies you can summon in the same way you do that to deepen your relationship with your spouse or friends whom you cherish.

At this juncture I must be frank to say that I do not understand "faith seeking understanding" as assent to and study of a set of propositions about God. What you want is not just to know *about* God; you want to know *God*, the *living* God, the Creator of the universe and the God of Abraham, Isaac, Jacob, and Jesus Christ. Faith is not faith in a set of propositions. Faith is not faith in the Bible. Faith is not faith in the inerrancy of the Bible. It is faith in the living God, which God awakens in you through the Holy Spirit and in which you grow through the love that God pours into your heart. Yes, the scriptures *are* the major record of the testimonies to God's self-disclosure, but how sad when some persons substitute studying the Bible or yelling about its inerrancy for getting to know the living God self-disclosed in that record. How sad, too, that their lives bear scant trace of the humbling, life-transforming effect of falling into the hands of the living God.

The Social Dimension

A healthy spirituality is never based on a lone ranger mentality. To enter into a relationship with the God of all humanity and all creation is to enter into a relationship with other human beings and with the world God has created. To enter into a relationship with God, the Father of Jesus Christ, moreover, is to enter into a relationship with the Body of

Christ—the humanity God is renewing in Christ, the people of God under a new covenant. More than that, it is to look at the world through God's eyes and to accept the role of the servant of God, to meet human need wherever or in whatever form you find it.

Accepting responsibility for the world, however, mandates maturity and wholeness. Not every child of God is ready to shoulder the burdens of others and to get deeply involved in the world's agonies, and no amount of exhortations or warnings or pleadings will suffice to persuade that person to do something that will make a difference. The life of Thomas Merton offers a good example on this point. People today may know Merton as one who wrote about the spiritual journey or as one of America's most perceptive social prophets. But he was not always one. When Merton entered the Abbey of Gethsemani in 1941, he pronounced a not very polite curse on the "world," clanged the doors shut, and vowed never to go back outside again to the place that had inflicted so much pain and that was scarred and torn by a war that would eventually claim sixty million lives. In the course of his formation in the monastery, Merton found that the "world" he sought so urgently to escape was in there with him. It came in with his "false self." At the same time as the publication of *The Seven Storey Mountain* made him a celebrity, he began to get different impressions of the world outside. A trip to Louisville on August 13, 1948, left him feeling that the city was "no longer so wicked after all." Merton mused, "Perhaps the things I resented about the world when I left it were defects of my own that I had projected upon it."[24] In February 1949, unable to work on a book, he wondered whether "the world I am sore at on paper is a figment of my own imagination."[25] Other reassessments followed wherein he began

---

[24] Thomas Merton, *The Sign of Jonas* (New York: Harcourt, Brace, & Giroux, 1979), 91.
[25] Ibid., 162.

to see that he had entered the monastery "to find my place in the world, and if I fail to find this place in the world I will be wasting my time in the monastery."[26]

During 1949 and 1950 Merton underwent an almost complete physical, spiritual, and emotional collapse, which he later labeled a "submarine earthquake." He also experienced a "rebirth" to the "world." He wrote in his journal on June 13, 1951, that he had "become very different from what I used to be. . . . Thus I stand on the threshold of a new existence. . . . For now I am a grown-up monk and have no time for anything but the essentials."[27] His next major writing was the wonderfully positive *No Man Is an Island*, whose very title heralded the change. In this series of essays he distinguished "true" from "false solitude."

> Both solitudes seek to distinguish the individual from the crowd. True solitude succeeds in this, false solitude fails. True solitude separates one [person] from the rest in order that he [or she] may freely develop the good that is his [or her] own, and then fulfill his [or her] true destiny by putting himself [or herself] in the service of everyone else. False solitude separates a [person] from his [or her] brothers [and sisters] in such a way that he [or she] can no longer effectively give them anything or receive anything from them in his [or her] own spirit.[28]

A couple of years after publication of this book, Merton recorded in his journal an experience of "awakening" from a period of spurious self-isolation on a trip to Louisville.

---

26 Ibid., 322.

27 Ibid., 329-30.

28 Thomas Merton, *No Man Is an Island* (New York: Harcourt, Brace, and Jovanovich, 1955), 248.

In Louisville, at the corner of Fourth and Walnut, in the center of the shopping district, I was suddenly overwhelmed with the realization that I loved all those people, that they were mine and I theirs, that we could not be alien to one another even though we were total strangers. It was like waking from a dream of separateness, of spurious self-isolation in a special world, the world of renunciation and supposed holiness. The whole illusion of a separate holy existence is a dream. Not that I question the reality of my vocation, or of any monastic life: but the conception of "separation from the world" that we have in the monastery too easily presents itself as a complete illusion: the illusion that by making vows we become different species of being, pseudo-angels, "spiritual men," men of interior life, what have you.

This sense of liberation from an illusory difference was such a relief and such a joy to me that I almost laughed out loud. . . . To think that for sixteen or seventeen years I have been taking seriously this pure illusion that is implicit in so much of our monastic thinking.

It is a glorious destiny to be a member of the human race, though it is a race dedicated to many absurdities and one which makes many terrible mistakes; yet, with all that God Himself gloried in becoming a member of the human race. A member of the human race! To think that such a commonplace realization should suddenly seem like news that one holds the winning ticket in a cosmic sweepstake.[29]

---

[29] Thomas Merton, *Conjectures of a Guilty Bystander* (Garden City, N.Y.: Image Books, 1968), 156-57.

Merton had at last gotten well enough and mature enough to embrace the world God made with all of its flaws.[30]

Social responsibility may be the best index of the level of maturity a Christian attains. Through the centuries, at any rate, saints have looked to what I call Jesus' parable of kingdom righteousness in Matthew 25:31-46 as the main guide. Matthew's chief theme is kingdom righteousness, inner goodness evidenced in outer character—good trees bearing good fruit (7:17-20); followers who *do* the will of God rather than simply say, "Lord, Lord" (7:21-23); and in the parable the downright good who feed the hungry, give drink to the thirsty, clothe the naked, visit the sick and imprisoned, and take strangers into their homes without even thinking about it. The mature in faith will do what is right unself-consciously because that is who they are. When the king invited them into the kingdom because they had done these things for him, they protested, "But when was it that we saw *you* hungry and gave you food, or thirsty and gave you something to drink?" He had to remind them that they were "just-as-ers": "Truly I tell you, just as you did it to one of the least of these who are members of my family, you did it to me" (25:40). To the spiritually mature, the other person, no matter who, is Christ!

Your major struggle as a believer today may be to extend your sense of responsibility to God's world in a technological age and culture that brutalize and wantonly waste nature and falter at making sacrifices that would avoid further and perhaps irreparable damage to the planet, for instance, as a consequence of global warming. Many today would think him awfully naive and simple, but Francis of Assisi pointed in the right direction. He put a face and a heart on nature when he praised God for "Brother Sun," "Sister Moon," "Mother Earth,"

---

30 For a fuller discussion see E. Glenn Hinson, "Contemptus Mundi-Amor Mundi: Merton's Progression from World Denial to World Affirmation," *Cistercian Studies* 26 (1991): 339-49.

and air, wind, and water—all creatures of our God and King. John Woolman, the American Quaker saint of the eighteenth century, discovered early a "principle" that it is contradictory "to say we love God as unseen, and at the same time exercise cruelty toward the least creature moving by [God's] life, or by life derived from [God]."[31] In a more sophisticated way than Francis but with the same intent, Teilhard de Chardin insisted that, "by virtue of the Creation and, still more, of the Incarnation, *nothing* here below is *profane* for those who know how to see."[32]

Spiritual maturity has to do with being sensitized and conscientized and tenderized to the presence of God in everything and everyone. It involves learning how to see beyond the external to the Eternal transecting time. That presence must surely have prompted Maltbie D. Babcock to write:

> This is my Father's world,
> and to my listening ears
> All nature sings, and round me rings
> the music of the spheres.

The Institutional Dimension

Many persons, especially baby boomers and Gen Xers, question whether the health of spirituality depends on institutional commitment and involvement. Baby boomers complain of "religious abuse" from the church, and as I have noted earlier, while displaying an intense interest in spirituality and community, they have a strong distaste for "religion," that

---

[31] John Woolman, *The Journal of John Woolman* (New York: Corinth Books, 1961), 8.

[32] Teilhard de Chardin, *Le Milieu Divin* (London: Fontana Books, 1962), 66.

is, institutional expressions of faith. A large percentage of seminarians balk at the thought of ministry in local congregations. Churches that many of these generations have attended now seem, in their present institutional patterns, ill equipped to do what God calls the church to do, that is to say, increase love of God and of neighbor. Can Christians not be more spiritual and live out their commitment to God better without institutions?

This is not a new question. It is one that has been raised again and again throughout Christian history, though perhaps not quite with the urgency with which that has occurred since the 1960s. Why, then, would von Hügel be so insistent on the importance of the institutional when he himself saw his own Roman Catholic Church jump with both feet on his modernist friends? The church prohibited even the burial of George Tyrrell, to whom von Hügel was especially close, in a Catholic cemetery; he was interred instead in an Anglican churchyard.[33] Why, too, would Thomas Merton remain in the Catholic Church when the National Conference of Catholic Bishops prohibited publication of his writings about peace during the Vietnam War? And why would he so meekly submit to his abbot at Gethsemani, James Fox, when the abbot imposed restrictions Merton considered patently unfair?[34]

The answers to these questions are quite complex, but two factors stand out for this discussion. First and foremost, both Baron von Hügel and Thomas Merton knew the importance of anchoring the spiritual life in a solid tradition. Nothing weakens faith more than to run off after the latest fad in religion, and nothing strengthens it more than to follow a path well marked out by tradition. Von Hügel and Merton were what might be

---

[33] David G. Schultenover, S.J., *George Tyrrell in Search of Catholicism* (Shepherdstown: Patmos Press, 1981), 356.
[34] See Thomas Merton, *A Vow of Conversation: Journals* 1964-1965 (New York: Farrar, Straus, & Giroux, 1988), 147-48.

called "unconventional traditionalists." As Merton defined tradition, it represents the essence, convention the external; tradition the kernel, convention the husk. You can discard convention, but you must remain faithful to tradition.[35]

You will find the same strong emphasis on tradition in a distinguished representative of the Free Church tradition, Douglas Steere. Quakers, like other Free Church groups, have a tendency to disconnect themselves from their roots in the contemplative tradition, and Douglas Steere, who did his doctoral dissertation on *Critical Realism in the Religious Philosophy of Baron Friedrich von Hügel* and published a volume on *Spiritual Counsel and Letters of Baron von Hügel*, took care to remind them of their connection with the Christian stream. Writing to a Swedish Friend about the relationship of Quakers to Jesus, he admitted that they had a problem here and proceeded to say,

> For me the Society of Friends is and must remain in the Christian stream. This means that the Bible and especially the Gospels must be read continuously by Friends and crossed with their own inward experiences. Dorothy and I try to read them together every morning and it is a good deal as the African said to his missionary guide, "Sir, it is not I who am reading the Bible. It is the Bible that is reading me!"[36]

Beyond the importance of tradition, all three of these recognized that institutions are essential to community. As Roman Catholics, von Hügel and Merton, of course, cherished

---

[35] On Merton's emphasis see E. Glenn Hinson, "The Catholicizing of Contemplation: Thomas Merton's Place in the Church's Prayer Life," *Perspectives in Religious Studies* 1 (spring 1974): 66-84.

[36] Douglas V. Steere, *letter to Sven Ryberg*, April 2, 1973; in E. Glenn Hinson, *Love at the Heart of Things*, 258.

the Mass in the way Steere, as a Quaker, could not. Merton, as a matter of fact, preferred the Latin Mass. Douglas Steere, however, was just as insistent on the meeting as they were on the Mass. We need community that comes to its most profound expression in gatherings for worship. In a pamphlet entitled On *Speaking Out of the Silence* Douglas Steere explained that Quakers come and sit in silence because they sense that "something is going on all the time, something we have only partially grasped the meaning of, and we long to be brought more deeply into touch with it." They come, too, "because we suspect that this communication may help us to discern what is being asked of us in the way of suitable action in the situation in which we stand and because we need strengthening in the power to carry this out."[37] The expected outcomes are twofold: yielding and being faithful. He chided Quakers for praying, "O God, teach us to do thy will—*to a certain extent*." A life open to God should result in obedience—"a sense of vocation, a living in the decision, a yielding to the *principle*, a coming under holy obedience or into devotion, a life of practice *in* the presence of God."[38]

Throughout Christian history the saints have recognized the serious failings and deficiencies of ecclesiastical institutions. Today we speak of such things as systemic evil and demonic structures. At the same time we have to recognize that Christianity is the most institution creating of all the world's religions and that we need structures to give order and meaning to our lives and to enable us to achieve what faith requires. No one trumpeted more loudly than Thomas Merton against "dead immobilism: the ponderous, inert, inhuman pressure of power bearing down on everyone to keep every beak from opening and

---

37 Douglas V. Steere, *On Speaking Out of the Silence*, Pendle Hill Pamphlet 182 (Wallingford, Pa.: Pendle Hill Publications, 1972), 6.
38 Douglas V. Steere, *The Open Life* (Philadelphia: Book Committee of the Religious Society of Friends, 1937), 4.

every wing from moving."[39] He fought through most of his religious life for "freedom to see and hear without self-imposed biases."[40] But Thomas Merton also recognized his need for structures in his religious development, so that Father Abbot James Fox could say at the time of Merton's death that, while he was the "most troublesome" monk he had ever had, he was also the "most obedient."[41]

Near the end of Merton's life, he fell in love with a nurse in a Louisville hospital where he had an extended stay. With the help of friends he arranged clandestine meetings with her. He wrote love letters and poems. He called her on the telephone. His secret remained unknown at the Abbey of Gethsemani for a while, but one morning about 2:00 A.M. one of the monks noticed a light on the switchboard, picked up the receiver, and heard Merton talking to his friend. Under obedience he reported to the abbot. The abbot immediately gave the order to stop. Merton obeyed.

None of this should be interpreted as overlooking the fact that at times you must take a prophetic stance that will pit you against the structures and powers that be. The prophets lifted up their voices against corrupted rites and rituals in ancient Israel. Jesus went to the cross because he posed a threat to the central institutions of his day—the Temple and the Law. Early disciples carried his protests farther. The monks, both men and women, went to the desert and bore their witness about the lapses of the church in times of peace. Here and there, reformers have organized their protests throughout Christian history. There is always the urgent issue of freedom for the word of God, of obeying God rather than other human beings (Acts 4:19). This,

---

[39] Thomas Merton, *Conjectures of a Guilty Bystander*, 228.

[40] So James Forest, "The Gift of Merton," *Commonweal*, January 10, 1969, 465.

[41] Quoted by Charles Dumont, "A Contemplative at the Heart of the World: Thomas Merton," *Lumen* 24 (1969): 634.

however, brings you back to the central thesis of this chapter, the importance of balance in spirituality. *Stand your spiritual life on four legs, not on one or two.* Each dimension—experiential, intellectual, social, and institutional—is essential to a healthy spirituality.

Chapter 7

SEXUALITY AND SPIRITUALITY

Sexuality raises important questions for spirituality. Too often in the past, however, sexuality has received negative notices with reference to the spiritual life. Sex can divert a person from devotion to God. Today you must recognize that you are a sexual being and that your sexuality has an important bearing upon your relationship with God, with other persons, and with the world around you. In this chapter I will address three questions relating to sexuality and spirituality as they bear on spiritual preparation for Christian leadership. How does sexuality affect your relationship with God? How does or should sexuality affect your relationship with other persons? How may sexuality contribute to spirituality?

Sexuality and Your Relationship with God

The answers to the question about how sexuality affects your relationship with God vary sharply.

Sex Seen as a Barrier to Intimacy with God

The conventional view, vigorously espoused since the time of Jerome (d. 420) and Augustine of Hippo (354–430), is that sex interferes with devotion and that true devotion demands celibacy. From an early date Christian authorities prohibited sex before Communion, looking upon it as at worst a defilement and at best a diversion for those renewing or strengthening their covenant with God. This prohibition paralleled the tradition concerning menstruation, also a reason not to receive Communion.

From the late second century, Christians advanced the view that sex is to be used only for procreation. The promiscuity so widely prevalent in Roman society influenced this view doubtless, but some in the early church also viewed the body as evil in a dualism that understood the spirit as good. Early Christian dualists carried their negativity toward the body in either of two directions—either uncontrolled indulgence or celibacy, both of which would show disdain for the body. Clement of Alexandria (ca. 160–211/16), the first to put forth the idea of sex-for-procreation-only,[1] did not espouse the radical dualism of other Gnostics, but he walked in their company. So, too, did his brilliant young disciple Origen. In an excess of devotion Origen castrated himself in order to become a "eunuch for the kingdom's sake" (Matt. 19:12, AP). Sex-for-procreation-only became and has remained the official teaching of the Roman Catholic Church.

Church thinkers elevated the status of virginity during the first several centuries. Tertullian of Carthage (ca. 160–225) listed a hierarchy of virtue: virginity from birth, virginity from

---

[1] Clement of Alexandria *The Instructor* 3.10. There are numerous translations of Clement and other patristic writers. I have cited those sources only when directly quoting these authors.

the new birth, continence in marriage, faithfulness in marriage.[2] As asceticism became more firmly rooted during the later third century and after, monks became models par excellence of the Christian life. Christian leaders more passionately underscored virginity as an essential ingredient of devotion. In 401 Pope Innocent I pronounced virginity "an indissoluble rule" for the clergy as well as monks.[3] Meanwhile, Jerome and Augustine took up the pen to undergird the conviction that true devotion, especially of Christian leaders, depended on renunciation of sex.

Jerome turned the issue into a crusade. A monk named Jovinian, supported by friends of Pelagius in Rome, argued that the celibate life is not superior to that of faithful marriage. Jerome suspected that Jovinian intended by that argument to disparage virginity and proceeded to set out the opposite position in a bitter diatribe entitled *Against Jovinian*. About the same time Jerome took up his cudgels *Against Helvidius* for suggesting that Mary was not perpetually a virgin but bore other children besides Jesus. Jerome wrote that those referred to in the scriptures as Jesus' "brothers" were actually his cousins.[4] Modern scholarship would support Helvidius, but Jerome had the backing of one of the most influential thinkers of Western history: Augustine of Hippo.

Augustine struggled to keep his libido under control during his early years. At age eighteen he entered into a liaison with a woman whose name he never mentioned in his published writings. She bore him a son whom they named Adeodatus, "given by God." Augustine then evidently joined the dualistic Manichaean sect in part because their explanation of evil salved his tender conscience on this issue. The Manichaeans conceived of evil as a corporeal substance, a kind of additive to human nature. He could not control his sexual impulses, they explained,

---

[2] Tertullian *Exhortation to Chastity* 1.1.

[3] Innocent I *Epistle* 2.

[4] Jerome *Against Helvidius* 11-19.

because of that additive. Their reasoning implied that Augustine acted in this way because he could not help it. For Augustine, conversion involved liberation from lust.

In his *Confessions* he recounted graphically his breakthrough in the little circle of companions who accompanied him to Cassiciacum, an estate outside Milan. Augustine heard Ponticianus tell the story of two young Roman noblemen who, on hearing that Anthony of Egypt gave up all of his possessions to follow Jesus as Jesus had instructed the rich youth (Matt. 19:16-30), abandoned their fiancées and assumed the life of hermits. This story created a crisis for Augustine. "You, O Lord, took me from behind my own back where I had hidden myself, since I did not want to look at myself," he confessed, "and stood me before my face that I might see how wicked I was, how twisted and evil, spotted and ulcerous. I looked and I was horrified. There was nowhere I could flee to from myself."[5] Every time he tried to find a way to escape, Ponticianus went on telling the story. Exasperated, Augustine stalked off into another part of the garden. He tried reading scriptures. That only increased his agitation. He hurled them to the ground and sought a still more secluded spot. There, in a while, he heard children playing some kind of game say, "Take up! Read! Take up! Read!" Understanding those words to be the voice of God, he hastened back to where he had thrown down the scriptures. They fell open at Romans 13:13-14: "Let us live in a fitting way, not in fights and drunkenness, not in sexual encounters and wantonness, not in strife and zeal, but put on the Lord Jesus Christ and no longer concentrate on the flesh for its lust." (author's translation) The word lust hit Augustine on his sorest sore. From that point, he and generations who looked to him for guidance in Christian life would intimately connect holy

---

5 Augustine *Confessions* 8.7.16, in *The Confessions of St. Augustine*, ed. John Gibb and William Montgomery, Cambridge Patristic Texts (New York and London: Garland Publishing, 1980), 219.

obedience, especially of the clergy, with avoidance of sex. We will explore later in this chapter the rather remarkable irony of the monastic use of the Song of Songs to interpret the monks' experience of God as they lived in celibacy.

Loving God Through Loving Others

At this point, however, you must ask whether there is not a healthier alternative to the preceding one. Can sex express and serve as a vehicle of devotion? Can you love God through loving another person? Or must your devotion to God take you away from your intimate friendship with another?

If you think of sex primarily in terms of the physical act of union, you may come down on the negative side on these questions. Self-serving indulgences of any kind do stand in the way of a relationship with God. If, however, you view it in the context of a love that unites persons in friendship, then you may make some sense of the monastic use of the Song of Songs. In fact, a twelfth-century Cistercian named Aelred of Rievaulx composed a remarkable treatise, *Spiritual Friendship*, that may help the case here. Although Aelred did not focus on sexuality, he looked upon friendship as a gift of God. God is love, and thus God reveals Godself in all forms of mutual attraction between human beings but especially in spiritual friendship. Equality, mutuality, and openness are the marks of such friendship. Whereas most monks thought that marriage stood in the way of mystical experience, for Aelred "spiritual friendship is both the model of the most direct experience of God and the way to attain the goal."[6]

The logical next step, then, is to recognize that you can love God through loving other persons. Indeed, if your goal is to love God in all that you do, loving another human being

---

[6] Bernard McGinn, *The Growth of Mysticism* (New York: Crossroad Publishing, 1996), 318.

selflessly, deeply, purely, and honorably would come very close to matching any experience of God that you can have in this life. Small wonder, then, that the mystics seized on the Song of Songs to help them interpret intimate experience of God.

Sex Not an Idol

Having said this, however, you do need to underline the adverbs selflessly, deeply, purely, and honorably. You live in a culture that encourages self-indulgence, self-centeredness, and egoism. This culture uses sex to sell its products and to establish priorities. It demeans and distorts sex by promoting it as an end in itself rather than as an expression of the highest form of love humans have for one another.

This points you to the need for *askesis*, discipline, in sex as in other things—food, drink, clothing, or pleasure of any kind. Sex is not to be an idol. You do not substitute sex for God. Surely, however great the pleasure you will derive from an intimate friendship, it cannot be as great as the pleasure of a friendship hallowed by and lived in God, the God who is Love.

Spirituality and the Sexual Aspect of Your Relationships

Spirituality can or should have a positive effect on the sexual aspect of your relationship with other persons. A healthy spiritual life should make you more sensitive, fully conscious, and tender in ways that would help you avoid abuse, diminish wrong attitudes and behavior, preserve sexual purity, and enhance sexuality. At the heart of spirituality are not spiritual exercises or methods but opening of the inner person to the increase of God's love "in understanding and in every sensitivity" (Phil. 1:9, AT). God's love works as no amount of human effort can.

Spirituality and the Problem of Sexual Abuse

Sexual abuse and harassment among Christian leaders are problems today, just as they are in American society in general. The Roman Catholic Church has experienced some of the most widely publicized and costly cases. In Massachusetts a former Roman Catholic priest pleaded guilty to sexual assault in molesting dozens of children thirty years before.[7] In New Mexico a Roman Catholic treatment center agreed to a multi-million-dollar settlement with twenty-five men who claimed to have been sexually abused by another former priest.[8] The Catholic Diocese of Dallas lost a $119.6 million lawsuit over the abuse of one priest and alleged attempts to cover it up.[9] The publicity stems from a response to the traditional teachings concerning celibacy. Less widely reported but no less scandalous are cases involving Protestant ministers, including United Methodist bishops as well as traveling evangelists who appear on television.

Some people assume that, because reports of sexual abuse have become commonplace, sexual abuse is a new problem generated by the greater openness and permissiveness today. It is not. Although contemporary attitudes may have opened the way to some abuses, the openness of the last half century has encouraged persons who were abused to speak about the unspeakable. Meantime, the notoriety of sexual abuse has emboldened legislators to pass laws protecting children and

---

[7] "Ex-Priest Pleads Guilty," *The Washington Post*, November 6, 1993.

[8] "Settlement for Ex-Priest's Accusers," *The Washington Post*, November 12, 1993.

[9] "Priest Enters Guilty Plea in 3 Sex-Abuse Charges," *The Richmond Times-Dispatch*, March 25, 1998.

women. Jurists hand down harsher or firmer sentences for offenses. Clergy as well as other counselors have found themselves charged with malpractice, harassment, and sexual abuse for offenses that an Elmer Gantry, a fictional clergyman, repeatedly committed without fear of punishment. The solution to the problem, however, is not stricter laws and harsher enforcement so much as the inward transformation of persons so that they will not be abusers and harassers.

Spirituality and Sensitivity to Others

Spiritual formation can help. The practices of spiritual formation make you more sensitive to others as individuals. In 1 Thessalonians 4:3-8 the Apostle Paul opened a new chapter in Western social history when he instructed husbands to treat their wives as persons and not as objects for their own sexual gratification. Paul's main point here is that husbands should not use their wives like prostitutes. Neither the RSV nor the NRSV rendering conveys Paul's main point. Puritan prudishness created a problem for both. The issue was not "how to take a wife for himself" (RSV) or "how to control your own body" (NRSV). A more accurate paraphrase is: "For this is God's will, your purity—that you avoid sexual license. Each of you husbands knows that you should engage in sex with your wife in purity and honor, not in uncontrolled lust such as the gentiles who do not know God do. [You know, too,] not to overstep the bounds and covet your brother's wife, just as we told you and attested before. For God did not call us to impurity but to purity."

Although this might seem obvious given the vantage point of two millennia of Christian history, such equality was not obvious to Paul's readers. Neither in Judaism nor in the Greco-Roman world were women regarded as persons. In Judaism a wife was the property of her husband. He could divorce her for almost any reason; she could not divorce him for any reason.[10] Aristotle, one of the luminaries of Greek philosophy, declared women inherently inferior to men.[11] In the upper classes in Roman society, senatorial or perhaps equestrian, women had certain rights, for example, regarding ownership of property, but the rights did not apply to women in the lower classes.[12] Here Paul places sensitivity to wives at the top of Christian behavior patterns—"the will of God." Husbands must abstain from fornication and engage their wives sexually "in purity and in honor, not in unbridled lust like the Gentiles who do not know God" (1 Thess. 4:3-5, AP). Paul adds a dire warning about God's judgment: "For God has called us not to uncleanness but in holiness. Therefore, anyone who disregards this does not disregard a human being but the God who gives [God's] Spirit to us" (vv. 7-8, AP).

First Peter 3:1-7 adds an interesting sidelight to the connection between husbands' attitudes toward their wives and spirituality. Portions of the text may not seem welcome to modern ears, but the main point can be well taken in the context of that culture and of our own. Husbands should pay due honor to their wives as being also the fellow heirs of a graceful life "so that your prayers may not be cut off" (1 Pet. 3:7, AP). Husbands who do not treat their wives with sensitivity manifest little of what a deep relationship with a God of love and grace should mean. As E. G. Selwyn remarked in his classic commentary, "Where hardening of heart is caused by lack of understanding in the highest and most delicate of all human relationships, the

---

[10] *Mishnah. Yebamot* 5.1-6.

[11] Aristotle *History of Animals* 9.1. In *Politics* 1.13 he establishes a case for the authority of freemen over slaves and men over women and children: "For the slave has no deliberative faculty at all; the woman has, but it is without authority, and the child has, but it is immature."

[12] See Jerome Carcopino, *Daily Life in Ancient Rome*, ed. Henry T. Rowell, trans. E. O. Lorimer (New Haven, Conn.: Yale University Press, 1940), 76-100.

relationship with God expressed in prayer is subject to serious impediment."[13]

The sensitivity I refer to is not limited to sexuality alone, but deals with the whole person. As modern psychological studies have demonstrated, sexuality belongs to your very nature as a human being and cannot be ignored in your relationships with other persons. To ignore sexual identity is to put yourself at risk of abusing and being abused by others. Like it or not, you relate to others as sexual beings.

Spirituality and Sexual Purity

Spirituality manifests itself in a concern for sexual purity and faithfulness to the covenants you enter into with others. The postmodern age has brought some powerful challenges to traditional understanding of sexual purity—sex only in the male-female married state. Today a large percentage of people do not wait until they are married to have their first sexual experience. Nearly fail-safe contraceptives have emboldened them. Even the threat of AIDS has not halted the trend; it has only raised the level of concern for "safe sex."

More open to dispute are same-gender relationships, particularly as they bear on worthiness for ministry. Conservative denominations such as the Southern Baptist Convention have not hesitated to condemn and to boycott the Disney Corporation for granting gay and lesbian couples the same job benefits as other couples. Southern Baptists would not think of ordaining gays and lesbians. The more liberal mainline denominations have found the issue divisive and not so simple. Of the mainline Protestant denominations, only the United Church of Christ accepts openly gay and lesbian individuals in

---

13 E. G. Selwyn, *The First Epistle of St. Peter* (London: Macmillan, 1949), 188.

ministry. Episcopalians,[14] Methodists,[15] and Presbyterians[16] have engaged in heated debate and not yet resolved the issue once and for all. Some denominations would ordain gays and lesbians who agreed to remain celibate but not those who engaged in an active sexual life.

No attempt can be made here to resolve this highly controverted issue, but spirituality offers some perspectives that are necessary to resolve the conflict. Spirituality insists, first of all, that God loves every person without regard to sexual preference or even, for that matter, behavior. (Consider God's worldly favorite, David!) In the New Testament you will find much weightier and more frequent denunciations of the wealthy than of homosexuality. Indeed, only twice does any word that can be construed as applying to active homosexuality appear in ethical lists (*arsenokoitai*, literally "sleepers with a male," in 1 Cor. 6:9 and 1 Tim. 1:10), and its meaning is debated. Nothing, surely, is more important than to imitate God's loving

---

[14] The debate in the Episcopal Church has revolved around ordination of gays or lesbians. Despite the expectation that candidates will abide by the church's condemnation of homosexual activity or sex outside marriage, the Episcopal Church has not prohibited ordination of homosexuals and some bishops have ordained them. See "Washington Bishop Ordains Lesbian as Priest," *Courier-Journal*, Louisville, Kentucky; June 6, 1991.

[15] The United Methodist Church has voted not to ordain active homosexuals, and the church has battled the issue for a quarter century. One Methodist pastor narrowly missed censure for "disobedience to the order and discipline of the United Methodist Church" for leading a ceremony in which two women exchanged rings and pledged their love to each other (*Christian Century*, April 1, 1998, 335-37).

[16] The issue of ordination of homosexuals has had an inordinate amount of attention in national assemblies of the Presbyterian Church (U.S.A.) in recent years. Since 1978 the church's policy has been not to ordain "self-affirming, practicing homosexuals," but many Presbyterians question how binding the policy is. See John P. Burgess, "Sexuality, Mortality and the Presbyterian Debate" *Christian Century*, March 5, 1997, 246-49, and "Presbyterians Keep Gay Ministers Ban," *Richmond Times-Dispatch*, March 19, 1998.

acceptance. If gender preference is innate and not learned, then you are especially challenged to rethink traditional attitudes and customs. Gay bashing is not acceptable.

Spirituality also makes humility the starting point of the spiritual life. Nothing more prohibitive stands in the way of your relationship with God than pride or self-righteousness. On the other hand, nothing opens access to God as does the plea, "God, be merciful to me, a sinner" (Luke 18:13). Benedict of Nursia[17] and Bernard of Clairvaux[18] viewed ascent of the "ladder of humility" as the necessary prelude to love of God. It is curious how some single out sexuality and turn it into an absolute when scriptures clearly make love of God and of neighbor the two great commandments!

Spirituality as an Enhancer of Sexuality

One further point needs to be added: Spiritual growth and development may make persons more attractive and, by increasing sensitivity, enhance this most intimate of all human relationships. To make this point, we should ask what most diminishes attractiveness to others. External appearance obviously enters into the equation. Self-esteem can be helped immensely sometimes by getting a new hairstyle, having a facelift, or even buying new clothes. Personality also plays a role. Negative personality traits will evoke responses from others that hurt badly. Over a long period, negative reactions can drive self-esteem into the ground. In the last analysis, however, low self-image clouds over the inborn attractiveness that you

---

[17] Benedict of Nursia *Rule* 7: "The ladder represents our life in this world, which our Lord erects to heaven when our heart is humbled."

[18] Bernard of Clairvaux, *The Steps of Humility and Pride* 1.1, declared: "The way is humility, the goal is Truth. The first is the labor, the second is the reward." Later (2.3) he asked, "What is this refreshment which Truth promises to those who climb and gives when they gain the top? Is it perhaps love itself?"

have to others. If that is so, growth of God's love in you can do most to head you in the opposite direction and enhance every aspect of your being, including sexuality.

Sexuality as an Aid to Spirituality

Sexuality has served and does serve as an aid to understanding the spiritual life just as spirituality aids sexuality. This may surprise or even startle you, but consider the analogy of intimacy in marriage that is used to interpret intimacy with God and in the use of feminine language and imagery to address God. In this section I want to address these. I do not think it is possible to consider these analogies apart from basic sexuality.

The Brautmystik *Tradition*

One of the two major traditions of Christian mysticism, the *Brautmystik* or Bridal Mysticism, has employed the love tryst between the newly married to help interpret the intimate relationship between God and the believer. The Song of Songs, which is clearly a magnificent poem describing lovemaking of bride and groom, has served from the time of Origen (185–254/5) as the scriptural warrant for this analogy. Although the sensuousness of the language and imagery may be shocking, it is not hard to understand why the analogy appealed to persons of profound religious experience or why they "spiritualized" it. The union of lovers can hardly be a purely physical act. Far from it. It is one of the most spiritual experiences of human beings.

Catherine Kapikian, artistic director, Center for the Arts and Religion, Wesley Theological Seminary in Washington, D.C., and a fabric artist, has expressed this point beautifully in a textile scheme she has designed for a Huppah (Jewish wedding canopy).[19] On the lower panel she has depicted the literal reading of the Song of Songs; on the upper panel, the spiritual reading. Human intimacy is both physical and spiritual. It engages the whole person. So, too, does loving God with heart, mind, soul, and strength!

In his *Commentary on the Song of Songs* Origen applied the words of the Lover to the Beloved in two ways—as Christ speaking to the church or to the individual soul. Others such as Gregory the Great (pope from 590 to 604), Bernard of Clairvaux, William of Saint-Thierry, Richard Rolle, and John of the Cross followed him in this, but they increasingly accentuated the more personal application. Their language sometimes reads like a Gothic romance. In this romance, however, they are talking about God and human beings. God, Christ, the Holy Spirit is the Lover who woos and wins the Beloved. The Beloved is aflame with love and is all atingle waiting for the union.

Bernard's "Jesus, the Very Thought of Thee," which graces virtually every modern hymnal, captures some of the soul's desire:

> Jesus, the very thought of thee
>   With sweetness fills my breast;
> But sweeter far thy face to see,
>   And in thy presence rest.
>
> No voice can sing, no heart can frame,
>   Nor can the mem'ry find
> A sweeter sound than Jesus' name,
>   O Savior of mankind!

---

[19] On Kapikian's work see Linda-Marie Delloff, "A Seminary's Artist in Residence: Cathy Kapikian's Fabric of Faith," *Christian Century*, March 18-25, 1987, 267-71.

O Hope of ev'ry contrite heart!
O Joy of all the meek!
To those who fall, how kind thou art!
How good to those who seek!

But what to those who find? ah! this,
No tongue or pen can show
The love of Jesus, what it is
None but his loved ones know.

Richard Rolle, the fourteenth-century English mystic and poet, emphasized affect to such an extent that Walter Hilton felt compelled to counter Rolle's influence *in The Scale of Perfection.* Rolle combined sensuous with musical imagery to express his longing for God.

O my Love! O my Honey! O my Harp! O my psalter and canticle all the day! When will You heal my grief? O root of my heart, when will You come to me so that You may raise up with You my spirit, looking upward for You? For You see that I am wounded vitally by Your super-brilliant beauty, and my lassitude does not release me. On the contrary, it rises greater and greater in its growth and present penalties press me and fight me, so that I hasten to You from Whom alone I hope for my comfort and the remedy about to be seen.[20]

Rolle's love poems, however, sound somewhat like some favorite hymns in Protestant hymnals.

Jesus, Jesus, Jesus,
For thee it is I long;

[20] Richard Rolle, *The Fire of Love and the Mending of Life*, trans. M. L. del Mastro (Garden City, N.Y.: Image Books, 1981), 224,

> Therefore, my life and my living,
> Thou art my only song.
> > Jesus, my dear and beloved,
> Delight art thou to sing;
> Jesus, my mirth and melody,
> When wilt thou come, my King?[21]

Not everyone has felt comfortable with the masculine language and imagery that have dominated Jewish and Christian God-talk. A study of the history of Israel helps in understanding a portion of the biblical perspective. The ancient Hebrews emphasized the maleness of Yahweh to counter the female deities of the Canaanite religions. Fertility was the major concern of the latter. Only rarely do you find some expression of the feminine side of God in the Hebrew or in the Christian Bible.[22]

The reticence to apply feminine imagery to God has not diminished greatly throughout Christian history, but one development merits comment, references to God and Christ as Mother. The early Christian Gnostics and the Montanists took a keen interest in the feminine, including women among their leaders. Thus, it is not surprising to find Clement of Alexandria among those who addressed Jesus as "Our Mother."[23] Irenaeus; Clement's successor, Origen; John Chrysostom; Ambrose; and Augustine also did this.[24] Fuller use of the address, however, did not occur until the twelfth century when Bernard of Clairvaux popularized it among Cistercians.[25]

Still more integral to an understanding of God comes from Julian of Norwich in the late fourteenth and early fifteenth

---

[21] *Selected Writings of Richard Rolle*, trans. John G. Harrell (London: SPCK, 1963), 38.

[22] See Phyllis Trible, *God and the Rhetoric of Sexuality* (Philadelphia: Fortress Press, 1978).

[23] Clement of Alexandria *The Instructor* 1.6.

centuries. "As truly as God is our Father," Julian (1343–after 1416) insisted, "so truly is God our Mother."[26] What Julian extracted from the fatherhood/motherhood of God was God's infinitely compassionate nature. A series of sixteen visions that she experienced in 1373 generated a buoyant optimism in an age that made grounds for optimism rare—the century of the Hundred Years' War, the bubonic plague, the Avignon papacy, and the papal schism. "Sin is necessary," she concluded, "but all will be well, and all will be well, and every kind of thing will be well."[27] What was the logic behind that? Years of reflection on the visions she had had of Christ led her to the conclusion that "love was his meaning."[28] The small thing "no bigger than a hazel nut" held in the hand of Christ showed the reason for optimism. "In this little thing I saw three properties," she explained. "The first is that God made it, the second is that [God] loves it, the third is that God preserves it. But what is that to me? It is that God is the Creator and the lover and the protector."[29]

The habits shaped by centuries of use make it difficult for some to modify their language and imagery, but for others it helps to salvage faith. God is neither male nor female in the sense in which that is true of human beings. What is important here is to exercise the freedom and discretion that will help you know how accessible God, your heavenly Parent, is. That is what has propelled the Christian search through the centuries.

---

24 See Caroline Walker Bynum, *Jesus as Mother: Studies in the Spirituality of the High Middle Ages* (Berkeley: University of California Press, 1981), 127.

25 Ibid., 111-13.

26 Julian of Norwich, *Showings*, trans. Edmund Colledge, O.S.A., and James Walsh, S.J., Classics of Western Spirituality (New York: Paulist Press, 1978), 295.

27 Ibid., 225.

28 Ibid., 342.

29 Ibid., 131.

Chapter 8

SUSTAINING THE SPIRITUAL LIFE, I:
SPIRITUAL READING, LISTENING, AND SEEING

Sustaining an intimate relationship with God is not easy in the demanding and fast-paced culture in which you live and work. Burnout, consumption of every ounce of spiritual energy to the point that you can no longer function with effectiveness, is an ever-present threat. By not paying enough attention to self-care, you may become a casualty of wounds self-inflicted from your dedication. The more devoted you are to the task, the more likely spiritual lethargy will overtake you to the extent that you will have nothing to offer the world that the world doesn't already have more of than it needs.

Keeping in touch with the working of grace in your life is, I think, the best way to think about your sustenance in the spiritual life. Grace is more than "God's unmerited favor," as Protestants have usually defined it. Augustine, a theologian of grace par excellence, spoke of it as a gift added to nature. Grace is God's gift of Godself, God's presence, the Holy Spirit. That surely is what Paul experienced in response to his plea for removal of his "thorn in the flesh" in 2 Corinthians 12:9, "My grace is sufficient for you." John Newton's universally favorite hymn "Amazing Grace" has a line in it that might well serve as the theme for the spiritual life of all Christians: "'Tis grace hath brought me safe thus far, and grace will lead me home."

The next three chapters will focus on some means for sustaining the spiritual life. They are based on a conviction that healthy spirituality requires balance of experiential, intellectual, social, and institutional dimensions and thus a variety of means. The present chapter will look at spiritual reading, listening, and seeing. Chapter 9 will underline the necessity of times of solitude and silence in preserving the spiritual life. Chapter 10 will highlight the importance of spiritual friendship.

Attentiveness to God

It seems appropriate to begin this reflection on sustaining the experiential dimension of the spiritual life by reminding you that attentiveness to God is the key. The goal is attentiveness in everything you are doing, whether spending time with the family, studying, preparing sermons, writing, visiting in the hospital, leading worship, organizing a community activity, marching to protest an injustice, or discharging the many other tasks in which a responsible leader engages. Humanly, though, you likely do not have the ability to sustain your attention without some periods of concentrated effort to raise the level of attentiveness. You may get caught up in activity for activity's sake and soon lose your way in the slough of busyness, even when that is for God. You need, therefore, deliberately to "spare some time for God," as the author of *The Imitation of Christ* exhorted.[1] Or perhaps you could say, "waste" some time for God and for yourself.

---

[1] *The Imitation of Christ* 1.20.

The peril facing you as a professional religious leader is doing everything for professional reasons and neglecting your personal relationship with God. You study scriptures to prepare sermons or to teach a Bible study. You read books or go to movies in order to find good sermon illustrations. You attend conferences and lectures to improve your various skills. At the same time you may let your personal covenant with God go begging.

In your deliberate attentiveness you must not forget that God may break through to you by way of all sorts of media. The range is unlimited. "Books and ideas and poems and stories, pictures and music, buildings, cities, places, philosophies," Thomas Merton remarked of his own life, "were to be the materials on which grace would work."[2] This means that you are well advised to keep alert to what Caussade called "the sacrament of the present moment." You do not want to miss "the One who is needful." At the same time Christians have always recognized that the canonical scriptures are more basic and dependable as means of grace than others. The scriptures come closer to giving you the words within which you may hear the word of God, revelation, than other writings. Even in their case, however, you have to apply yourself to the task of paying attention to the working of grace in your life.

Experiencing Grace Through Scriptures

The first place you may expect to encounter grace is through scriptures. Through the centuries the most basic form of prayer has involved meditation on the scriptures. The Protestant Reformers and their offspring thought they had recovered the

---

2 Thomas Merton, *The Seven Storey Mountain* (New York: Harcourt, Brace, Jovanovich, 1948; 1976), 178.

use of scriptures, but what they really did was to put an end to monastic and clerical monopoly on their use and to place scriptures at the center of Protestant devotion. The Reformers spoke of themselves as "people of one Book." Unfortunately, at the same time, those first Protestant leaders cast overboard many of the well-tried and proven methods of meditation, a practice that impoverished the spiritual life of their descendants. Puritans and Pietists had to help recover many of those practices.

I wish to emphasize at this juncture the importance of Christian leaders' personal discipline. The Benedictine *Opus Dei* took roughly four hours for the eight times monks gathered to chant the Psalms. In addition, Benedictines spent another four hours in the *lectio*, which entailed chiefly meditation on scriptures. Martin Luther spent three hours a day in prayer. During his turbulent struggle with manic depression, John Bunyan pored over the scriptures. He wrote in *Grace Abounding* that "indeed, I was then never out of the Bible, either by reading or meditation; still crying out to God that I might know the truth, and way to heaven and glory."[3] During his imprisonment, his musings about "religionless Christianity" notwithstanding, Dietrich Bonhoeffer spent many hours in prayer and held a high view of its importance. "I think I owe it to the prayers of others, both known and unknown, that I have often been kept in safety," he said to his brother-in-law, Eberhard Bethge.[4]

Although few busy leaders in less critical circumstances would commit those amounts of time to meditation on the scriptures today, at least thirty minutes a day seems essential. Bonhoeffer required the seminarians at Finkenwalde, the school begun in 1935 to prepare clergy for the Confessing Church, to

---

[3] John Bunyan, *Grace Abounding to the Chief of Sinners*, in Doubleday Devotional Classics, edited by E. Glenn Hinson (Garden City, N.Y.: Doubleday & Co., Inc., 1978), I, 230.
[4] Dietrich Bonhoeffer, *Letters and Papers from Prison*, enlarged edition ed. Eberhard Bethge (New York: Macmillan Publishing Co., 1953), 392.

spend thirty minutes each morning meditating on the same passage of scriptures for a week. They needed to wrestle with just one passage, he explained, until it blessed them. The rest of the day they were to apply themselves to their work. Finding behind the "it" of work the "Thou," which is God, he added, is what Paul meant when he spoke of "praying without ceasing."[5]

Experiencing Grace Through Other Writings

In addition to scriptures, however, other writings, not only devotional ones, enable people to discover God's grace. Cicero's *Hortensius*, a work now lost, led Augustine to what many scholars label his "first conversion," at age eighteen. Coming into his hands two years after his father died, *Hortensius* did far more than sharpen his rhetorical skills. Augustine wrote, "This book changed my affections. It turned my prayers to you, Lord, and caused me to have different purposes and desires. All my vain hopes forthwith became worthless to me, and with incredible ardor of heart I desired undying wisdom. I began to rise up, so that I might return to you."[6]

John Bunyan, though a person of one book like other Puritans, found grace not only in scriptures but in other writings. Two books that challenged him powerfully were the popular Puritan manuals of Arthur Dent (*The Plain Man's Pathway to Heaven*) and Lewis Bayly (*The Practice of Piety*). More

---

5 Dietrich Bonhoeffer, *Life Together*, trans. John W. Doberstein (New York: Harper & Brothers, Publishers, 1954), 70-71.

6 *The Confessions of St. Augustine*, trans. John K. Ryan (Garden City, N.Y.: Image Books, 1960), 81.

important in helping Bunyan rise above his depression was Martin Luther's *Commentary on Galatians*. Reading only a little way in it, Bunyan wrote, "I found my condition, in his experience, so largely and profoundly handled, as if his book had been written out of my heart." Significant of his own high esteem, he went on to add, "I do prefer this book of Martin Luther upon the Galatians (excepting the Holy Bible) before all the books that ever I have seen, as most fit for a wounded conscience."[7]

Thomas Merton, wide ranging in his literary interests, discovered the operation of grace through many and varied writings. Early on, he encountered William Blake and fell captive to him. "I think my love for William Blake had something in it of God's grace," he said of this romance in *The Seven Storey Mountain*. "It is a love that has never died, and which has entered very deeply into the development of my life."[8] In Etienne Gilson's *The Spirit of Medieval Philosophy* he encountered a concept, that of God's self-existence (aseity), "that was to revolutionize my whole life."[9] The Hindu Bramachari guided him to two other writings, Augustine's *Confessions* and *The Imitation of Christ*, which also impacted him profoundly.

In his *Thoughts in Solitude* Merton wrote that books may affect us in different ways. They "can speak to us like God, like men [or women] or like the noise of the city we live in."[10] In part that is true because of their content. Some books are only the noise of the city. Others engage you in deeply personal ways.

---

7 John Bunyan, *Grace Abounding*; The Doubleday Devotional Classics, edited by E. Glenn Hinson (Garden City, N.Y.: Doubleday & Co., Inc., 1978), I, 250-251.

8 Merton, *The Seven Storey Mountain*, 122.

9 Ibid., 172.

10 Thomas Merton, *Thoughts in Solitude* (New York: Farrar, Straus and Giroux, 1956, 1958), 62.

In still others God speaks. In part, this is true because of what is going on in you. Sometimes you are so full of the noise of the city that some of the grandest passages in all scriptures will sound like discord. On those occasions you have to become inwardly quiet as you attend to God.

How do you read devotional classics so as to gain the most edification from them? Very much as you do scriptures, as the *lectio divina* of the Benedictine tradition teaches you. Try this approach:

1. *Make a selection.* Not every writing listed as a classic will be equally helpful to everyone. More recently written classics may be easier to read and to draw insights from; however, using only modern writings would cause you to miss some of the world's most profound and beneficial spiritual guides. There is much to be said for ranging more widely, perhaps taking advantage of some guides to Christian devotional classics such as *Doors into Life*,[11] *Seekers after Mature Faith*,[12] or *Christian Spirituality*.[13] You may wish to browse the sixty volumes of the Classics of Western Spirituality.

It may be somewhat presumptuous to narrow such an extensive list, but to gain insight into the spiritual life, you may want to consider the following: Augustine's *Confessions*; Benedict of Nursia's *Rule; The Little Flowers of St. Francis*; *The Imitation of Christ*; Julian of Norwich's *Showings*; Ignatius Loyola's *Spiritual Exercises;* Teresa of Avila's *Life* and *The Interior Castle*; John of the Cross's *The Dark Night of the Soul*;

---

[11] Douglas V. Steere, *Doors into Life through Five Devotional Classics* (New York: Harper & Row, 1948), treats five classics in depth.

[12] E. Glenn Hinson, *Seekers after Mature Faith* (Waco, Tex.: Word Books, 1968), is a historical introduction, giving the background and summarizing the content of most of the recognized classics.

[13] *Christian Spirituality*, ed. Frank N. Magill and Ian P. McGreal (San Francisco: Harper & Row, 1988), gives a brief blurb on the author and summarizes the content of each classic.

John Bunyan's *Grace Abounding* and *The Pilgrim's Progress*; Pascal's *Pensées*; Brother Lawrence's *The Practice of the Presence of God*; William Law's *A Serious Call to a Devout and Holy Life*; John Woolman's *Journal*; Søren Kierkegaard's *Purity of Heart*; Teilhard de Chardin's *The Divine Milieu*; Bonhoeffer's *The Cost of Discipleship, Life Together*, and *Letters and Papers from Prison*; Alfred Delp's *Prison Meditations*; Thomas Kelly's *A Testament of Devotion*; Douglas Steere's *On Beginning from Within* and *On Listening to Another*; Thomas Merton's *The Seven Storey Mountain, Thoughts in Solitude, New Seeds of Contemplation*, and *Conjectures of a Guilty Bystander*; Dag Hammarskjöld's *Markings*; and Elie Wiesel's *All Rivers Run to the Sea*.

Although this list includes writings essentially of a devotional character, it is important not to limit the list of books or poems or stories through which God may touch your life. As in Augustine's case, writings not of Christian connection may have the deepest impact in certain circumstances.

2. *Learn all you can about the historical background of the classic.* The older classics' insights may not break through clearly until you know something about the historical context—author, date and place of writing, purpose, and the like. In some cases you cannot get accurate and definite information. *The Imitation of Christ*, for instance, almost certainly went through an editorial process before it reached its present form. Originally compiled as a handbook for persons entering the Brothers of the Common Life, *The Imitation of Christ* may have been written by the founder of that movement, Geert de Groote. Thomas à Kempis, identified in many manuscripts as the author, was probably the final editor. Knowing this information may help you to understand and appreciate *The Imitation* in the same way such information helps you to interpret a Bible passage.

3. *Read the classic in a leisurely fashion, and reread it.* These works contain deep insights that you will not dig out in

hurried reading. In the *lectio divina* the monks paused frequently to let the ideas soak in. They thought of the *lectio* as analogous to a cow chewing its cud. The cow chews, swallows, and then belches back up the hay to chew it again.

Classics, like scriptures, also require rereading. Some of the genuine gems will remain hidden on first reading and jump out of hiding later. One of the incalculable benefits of teaching the classics year after year, which I have done for more than thirty years, is the fresh insight each new group of students may find when they make a presentation on a particular classic. Changing times and circumstances put each writing under a different light. Little by little, that light will illumine the depths of your inner being if you persist in your reading.

4. *Relate the insights of the classics to your life and work today.* Classics probably attain classic status because, as Bunyan said about Luther's *Commentary on Galatians*, you find your condition in the experience of their authors dealt with in such a profound way that it sounds as if they had written from your own heart. Although all writings are conditioned by their time and circumstances, these particular works transcend the centuries in probing God's involvement in human experience and how you may live out your commitment to God in all of life. There remains for you the task of assimilating these profound discoveries and letting them fill your whole existence.

Some classics will not demand much effort on your part. They will zoom in on your wavelength finely tuned to where you are at the moment. Many readers of Thomas Kelly's *A Testament of Devotion* will attest that of it. Kelly's book is replete with simple yet profound guidance to God's accessibility and human responsibility. Grasping the insights mentally, however, is not the same as taking them into your heart.

Experiencing Grace Through Other Media

Literature is not the only means through which postmoderns can experience the working of grace in our lives. Our culture has been in a transition comparable to and perhaps greater than the one begun with Gutenberg's invention of movable type. Whereas European culture, especially Protestant culture, shifted from a predominantly iconic and tactual to a more typographic style, our culture is shifting from a predominantly typographic to a more iconic and tactual style. Beginning in the sixteenth century, Protestantism has relied especially on the written and spoken word and less on sacraments and images. Now that process is reversing. We still learn from the written and spoken word, but we are now making much more use of sight and touch.[14]

Behind this significant change stands the vast technological revolution of the last century. Movies, television, and computers have helped us think in more symbolic and graphic ways. Neil Postman has pointed out in *Amusing Ourselves to Death* that students who grew up with Sesame Street still want Sesame Street in the classroom. Speakers rely on "sound bites" to reach their hearers, not on carefully structured argument. Preachers dare not try the three-hour sermons of their Puritan ancestors. Politicians promote their campaigns largely through projecting an image rather than relying on stated public philosophies. Readers prefer the digest approach of *USA Today* to the analytical approach of the *New York Times* or *Washington Post*. Most television news programs

---

[14] In brief essays that I asked students in one of my classes to write on the topic "How I Learn," they listed the following factors: (1) hands-on involvement, (2) impact of a teacher, (3) trial and error, (4) memorization and repetition, (5) association and organization of information, (6) motivation, and (7) visual aids. The most consistent emphasis rested on hands-on involvement and visual aids.

focus on human interest and commentary rather than a factual reporting of events.

Although the revolution has a downside in that television aims at entertainment and threatens to create an "entertainment culture,"[15] these new ways of thinking contribute positively to the sustaining and uplifting of the spiritual life. In the same way that you think of a global culture, you begin to gain a sense of a global Christian spirituality. You gain a more wholistic approach to the working of grace in your life. Your senses may assist you. Consider these approaches:

Seeing

Art is a powerful medium of grace, and some of the world's greatest works of art arose out of religious inspiration. The art of the churches of Rome deeply affected Thomas Merton at age eighteen. In Rome's Byzantine mosaics Merton found "an art that was tremendously serious and alive and eloquent and urgent in all that it had to say."[16] For the first time in his life, Merton "began to find out something of Who this Person was that [people] called Christ." Though he could not decode all he saw, "the realest and most immediate source of this grace was Christ Himself, present in those churches, in all His power, and in His Humanity, in His Human Flesh and His material, physical, corporeal Presence."[17] Merton's visit to those churches set him up for an experience of the presence of his father, who had died just three years before, which "overwhelmed [him] with a sudden and profound insight into the misery and corruption of [his] own soul." This experience formed prayer anew in Merton: "Not with my lips and with my

---

15 Neil Postman, *Amusing Ourselves to Death: Public Discourse in the Age of Show Business* (New York: Penguin Books, 1986), 87.

16 Merton, *The Seven Storey Mountain*, 108.

17 Ibid., 110.

intellect and my imagination, but praying out of the very roots of my life and of my being, and praying to the God I had never known, to reach down towards me out of His darkness and to help me to get free of the thousand terrible things that held my will in their slavery."[18]

You may discover icons as part of your spiritual discipline. Keeping focused on God often persists in prayer. Your mind wanders and recollects other matters. Icons help center attention on God. Icons were never intended as objects of worship; their purpose, rather, was to direct the believer beyond the image to God. That was the reason they were painted two-rather than three-dimensionally. Your gaze should pass through the surface image to the Trinity.

I must be frank to deal here with a problem that the Reformers created when they insisted that their followers be "people of the Book." The Reformed tradition in particular viewed art with suspicion as a violation of the second commandment. John Calvin replaced the stained glass windows of St. Peter's in Geneva with plain glass. During the English Civil War (1642–46), the Roundheads of Cromwell's army, who evidently comported themselves in admirable ways otherwise, could scarcely pass a stained glass window of the Madonna and Child without throwing rocks to break the window. Protestants influenced by this tradition have moved slowly and cautiously to recognize that icons, paintings, mosaics, statuary, stained glass, architecture, and other visuals might be sacramental, that is, means of grace.

Architecture, too, may contribute to your awareness of the presence of God in the midst of life. The soaring spires of Salisbury Cathedral symbolically linking heaven and earth, the four-tiered and golden-domed St. Basil's in the Kremlin, and the overstated baroque of St. Peter's in Rome speak eloquently in

---

18 Ibid., 111.

their different ways of the double search—humankind's reaching out toward God and God's relentless pursuit of humankind. Protestants had to make a long pilgrimage backward to discover that, though God is not confined to place, we may not worship in barns as readily as we may in structures we have raised up with love and care and attention to worship.

Contemporary **movies** may touch you with deeply spiritual messages. Some films that have been revelatory to me include Dead Man Walking, Little Women, To Kill a Mockingbird, Steel Magnolias, A River Runs Through It, Nell, Priest, and Schindler's List. These may entertain, as movies are designed to do, but they do far more than that. Each wrestles with issues of faith, hope, and love from a different perspective. As in the reading of books, whether you may derive spiritual nourishment from films may depend on whether you come equipped with a contemplative outlook or simply seek entertainment.

Touching, Tasting, and Smelling

Western culture today is not only more iconic; it is also more tactual or tactile. People want more hands-on experience. They are not content merely to hear about something. They want to "see" it for themselves, do it themselves. Students, for instance, want to travel to the places whose history they are studying and meet the people whose culture they want to understand, for the technological revolution of the past century has made such travel altogether feasible.

In earlier centuries sacraments met tactual needs. Early Christians, for instance, promised the anxiety-ridden of their day tangible assurance of participation in Christ's victory over demons, forgiveness of past sins, rebirth or regeneration, illumination, and hope of eternal life through baptism and the Lord's Supper. They replaced expensive offerings of bulls or goats in competing religions with the Lord's Supper or Eucharist, which they called "the *unbloody* sacrifice." In the West during the Middle Ages the Mass increased in importance as churches sought to meet the needs of the diverse Germanic peoples who controlled Europe. The clergy, mostly monks, offered masses for all sorts of things--to cure cattle and people of their diseases, to protect pilgrims in their travels, to improve weather conditions, to secure victory in battle, and to strengthen souls in the battle with the demonic. The demand for masses necessitated the construction of altars in the side aisles of the churches because a single altar would not suffice to meet the demand. The church also expanded the number of sacraments to seven--baptism, confirmation, Eucharist, penance, marriage, ordination, and anointing of the sick or extreme unction—in order to cover the crucial passages of life.

Thanks to actions taken in the Council of Trent (1545–63), the whole sacramental system has remained vital in the Roman Catholic Church. Renewed emphasis on scriptures and the sermon at the Second Vatican Council (1962–65) has shifted the weight slightly toward the typographic but has not diminished the iconic and tactual inherited from the medieval church. In Protestantism, however, the shift was far more severe, especially in the Reformed and radical traditions. Although the magisterial Protestant Reformers still defined the church as "where the Word is rightly preached and the sacraments properly administered," they weighted the reform far more heavily toward the typographic in rejecting the system of seven sacraments and the Mass. Scriptures and sermon became the chief sacraments for the Reformers. Scriptures and sermon were the means of grace. Protestantism today will have a steeper climb to adjust to the more recent cultural revolution involving senses beyond hearing.

The ecumenical revolution that Pope John XXIII (1958–63) set in motion offers guidance to Protestants, for we are now able to learn from one another in ways not previously possible. What stands out noticeably is a kind of "holy discontent" that younger generations of Protestants feel about the wordy worship of many Protestant churches. Such worship fails to engage and involve them in the way of Roman Catholic, Orthodox, or Anglican worship. The thinness of denominational walls makes it convenient for many, even ministers, to sample the wares in traditions other than their own.

Satisfaction for your tactual needs, however, may come from sources other than sacraments, for, as Elizabeth Barrett Browning reminded long ago, "All the world's alive with God, and every bush is a burning bush." The universe is, for those who know how to "see," sacramental. Nature opens what Rufus Jones called "the soul's east window of divine surprise."[19] You are meant by God to be a citizen of two worlds—a space/time world and a world of spiritual values. As a citizen of those two worlds, you might call yourself an "amphibian." This could mean gazing in awe as the sun rises, hiking the Appalachian Trail, fishing in a trout stream, lying on your back and looking up at the stars. It could involve taking part in haying, harvesting grain, milking cows, currying horses. It could take the form of woodworking, clock making, refinishing furniture, building houses with Habitat for Humanity. Or it may focus on contact with other persons—such as Mother Teresa of Calcutta, seeking the face of God in the poorest of the poor, loving and serving Christ in "his distressing disguise."[20] "Do not underestimate our practical means—the work for the poor, no matter how small or humble—that make our life something beautiful for God."[21]

---

19 Rufus Jones, *A Preface to Christian Faith in a New Age* (New York: Macmillan, 1932), 56.
20 Mother Teresa, *My Life for the Poor*, ed. José Luis González-Balado and Janet N. Playfoot (San Francisco: Harper & Row, 1985), 95.
21 Michael Collopy, *Works of Love Are Works of Peace: Mother Teresa of Calcutta and the Missionaries of Charity* (San Francisco: Ignatius Press, 1996), 198.

Chapter 9

SUSTAINING THE SPIRITUAL LIFE, II:
SEEKING SOLITUDE AND SILENCE

The spiritual life will not remain vital without solitude and silence. Solitude ends the ceaseless bombardment of your senses by external stimuli and permits you again to become collected. As Douglas Steere observed years ago, all too many persons in our society suffer from uncollectedness. The uncollected, which all of us are sometimes, are persons constantly pressed for time. They have no time for private prayer or leisurely reading, reflecting, or setting down thoughts; they are impatient and thus crowd decisions and squeeze and maneuver other people. Uncollected people are likely to talk and not listen. They operate according to their own plan with little attention to others. Collected people are, by contrast, persons "glad to have time to spare for God" and for others; are really present to others and not pining to be some other place; have time to look at the stars; are capable of being patient; are not afraid to sleep because they are grounded "in One whose triumph is already established." Such people are not utterly planless but have "a certain sense of seeing the things that happen to [them] over against eternity and, therefore, to catch something of the vast humor in their curiously crooked incongruity against that setting." Although collected persons are also divided, they know the source of the division and the way to heal it, that is, through prayer.[1] Citing Caroline Stephens, Douglas Steere remarked elsewhere that "solitude is the stronghold of the strong." It is not a matter of "finding time" for it but of "the depth of the sense of need and of the desire."[2]

The object of solitude is silence. By that I mean not just removal of yourself from external noises but an interior quiet freed from the noise and franticness that skew your life and keep you from being who you are. Silence allows you to hear "the still, small voice" (1 Kings 19:12) vying for your attention. You need that time to open yourself more fully to God as you engage with the world around you.

In referring to this need for solitude and silence, I propose retreats. The word retreat derives from the Latin *retrahere*, which means "to draw back." Retreat should not be seen as a "flight from the world" pronouncing a not very polite curse on it, as some Christians have occasionally seen it. Not even the monastic retreat, in its true form, intended that. Quite to the contrary, the early monks sought solitude for the same reason Jesus did—to get in touch with One who brought the world into being and who directs the world toward some meaningful end.

The Gospels, especially Luke, report that Jesus spent

---

[1] Douglas V. Steere, "On the Collected and Uncollected Man," sermon, First Presbyterian Church, Tallahassee, Florida, January 22, 1961. Summary drawn from E. Glenn Hinson, *Love at the Heart of Things: A Biography of Douglas V. Steere* (Wallingford, Pa.: Pendle Hill Publications; Nashville, Tenn.: Upper Room Books, 1998), 261.

[2] Douglas V. Steere, *Prayer and Worship* (New York: Hazen Books on Religion, 1938), 17.

time in retreat before each of the critical moments of his ministry. After his baptism and before he began his public ministry, Jesus spent forty days in the wilderness (Matt. 4:1-11; Mark 1:12-13; Luke 4:1-14). After his temptation and the launch of his ministry (Luke 4:1-16), Jesus "went to a desert place" to pray (Mark 1:35-38; Luke 4:42-43). Before choosing the Twelve, "he went out to the mountain to pray and spent all night in prayer to God" (Luke 6:12, AP; cf. Matt. 10:1-4; Mark 3:13-19). Before the revelation at Caesarea-Philippi, Luke says, "he was praying alone" (Luke 6:12, AP). When the disciples came to ask him to teach them how to pray, they found him praying (Luke 11:1-4; cf. Matt. 6:9-13). As the critical conclusion to his ministry drew near, he retreated to the Garden of Gethsemane to pray (Matt. 26:36-41; Mark 14:32-38; Luke 22:39-46).

Many Protestants, convinced that the Christian life must justify itself by what it achieves, find it difficult to understand that some persons have experienced a calling to solitude and a life of prayer. The first students I took to visit a monastery did not understand that calling. I confess that I arranged the visit to expose them to the Middle Ages and not to learn about prayer as the monastic vocation. Thomas Merton, our host, gave us more than we expected. After talking about monastic life, Merton asked if there were questions. One student asked what I most feared would be asked, "What is a smart fellow like you doing in a place like this?" I expected Merton to respond in anger or in frustration that he had not been heard, but Merton replied very simply: "I am here because this is my vocation. I believe in prayer."

Will all of us have to go into monasteries or enter religious orders to find solitude and silence? Or seek our own "Walden Pond" where we will not have to confront the world's interruptions and disruptions? Surely not. Not many today, at least, sense a vocation to such places. All can find solitude. All can benefit from what persons such as Thomas Merton have found in their vocation. In an article entitled "The Contemplative Life: Its Meaning and Necessity," Merton wrote that, although the contemplative life is normally lived in monasteries, "in a broader sense every life can be dedicated to some extent to contemplation, and even the most active of lives can and should be balanced by a contemplative element—leavened by the peace and order and clarity that can be provided by meditation, interior prayer and the deep penetration of the most fundamental truths of human existence."[3]

Where and how, then, are you as a Christian leader to find solitude and the silence you must have in order to be sustained in ministry? The *where* is easier to answer than the *how*. Just everywhere. In your home. In your car traveling to work or on vacation. In your office. Even in the midst of other people. The desert fathers and mothers always urged their fellows to hurry back to their cells. "Fish, if they tarry on dry land, die," one of them cautioned. "Even so monks that tarry outside their cell or abide with [people] of the world fall away from their view of quiet."[4] Those experienced in the life of prayer, however, knew that the cell did not guarantee concentration on God. One of the desert Ammas wisely said, "It is better to have many about thee, and to live the solitary life in thy will, than to be alone, and the desire of thy mind be with the crowd."[5] Your thoughts can just as readily distract you when you are alone as when you are with others.

How you find solitude, as Douglas Steere has remarked, will doubtless depend on the depth of your sense of need and of your desire more than on external circumstances, however important they are sometimes. You will likely discover that,

---

3 Thomas Merton, "The Contemplative Life: Its Meaning and Necessity," *Dublin Review* 223 (winter 1949): 26-35.

4 Abba Antony *The Sayings of the Fathers* 2.1, in *The Desert Fathers*, trans. Helen Waddell (Ann Arbor: University of Michigan Press, 1977), 63.

5 The Abbess Matrona *The Sayings of the Fathers* 2.14; Waddell, 66.

although you want to make all of life a prayer, you will require some focused times of attention to God and yourself in order to maintain such perspective in a culture, including a church culture, that insists on grabbing so much of your attention for itself. Stated in the briefest way, you will need *daily* retreats, *monthly* or perhaps even *weekly* retreats, *longer* retreats—thirty-six to forty-eight hours or more—twice a year, and sabbaticals.

Daily Retreating

The idea of a *daily* retreat may seem a little strange. You may be accustomed to irregular and infrequent times of solitude and silence. In the case of a Christian leader, it is important that you begin to raise the profile on your need for regular and frequent attention to God if you are not only to survive but also to bring to the lives of others what really matters. All too many leaders are like depleted car batteries trying to turn a heavy engine in the dead of winter; they make a little noise, but they don't have enough energy to fire up the lifeless engine. And the more dedicated the ministers, the more likely they will be to have worn down the battery trying to start the car.

How do you conduct a daily retreat? The answer depends on how you can best find the solitude and silence in which you can pay attention to God. The one essential would appear to be *discipline*. People in ministry often make excuses to God: "Oh, God, you understand that I'm doing your business. I just don't have time to stop and pay attention. I have an endless number of things to do—a sermon to write, umpteen hospital calls and people to visit, meetings to attend, funerals to conduct. You should understand."

Does God understand? Does God accept such excuses? Maybe. God is forgiving of most human failures and foibles. But the prophets of the Hebrew Bible, John the Baptist, Jesus, and the Evangelists of the New Testament do not seem to have thought that God kindly overlooked the inattention of religious leaders that resulted in the pretending of faith rather than faithful practice. Matthew recorded a basketful of "woes" on scribes and Pharisees for an external piety that resulted in hypocrisy, religion "to be seen of other persons": showboating religion, loading heavy burdens on others that they would not touch (23:1-7); seeking the preeminence of rabbis rather than being servants (23:8-12); swearing by the Temple rather than letting their word be their bond (23:16-22); tithing with exactitude but neglecting the weightier matters of the Law (23:23-24); cleansing the outside of the cup and whitewashing tombs but neglecting the inside (23:25-28); and building tombs to honor the prophets they had killed (23:34-36).

Suppose that you decide to schedule focused times of attention to God. What do you do with them? My own method, if I can call it that, is to walk three miles every morning before breakfast. I can't describe exactly what I do because I do not have a set routine. Some days I just walk. Some days I am overcome with awe as our great fiery sun comes up over the horizon. Some days I meditate on a passage or passages of scriptures. Some days I intercede for someone or pray about some concern. I can tell you what results from this time of solitude and attentiveness: I am collected. I am present where I am, really present, not just halfway present. As a consequence, I get more done. My writing is deeper. My relationship with those around me is more satisfying for all.

Douglas Steere began his day with thirty minutes of silence perhaps preceded by reading of a passage of scriptures, usually from the Gospels. You can do this anywhere—at home, in a hotel room, in an office, wherever you find yourself. Just be there, coming without any agenda. You are stepping into an already flowing stream whose source is God. Douglas has described what happens in this way:

It is hard for me to underline sufficiently what a difference it makes to enter prayer with a deep consciousness of this divine initiative. To be conscious that long before I make my response in prayer at all, something immensely costly and penetrating has been going on. That it continues during my prayer and that it continues to undergird my very life when I have turned from conscious acts of prayer to my other tasks of the day. This and nothing short of this gives my prayer its true setting. Prayer is a response to God's "is-ness." My prayer did not begin this encompassing love. That love has been like a poultice laid over me and laid over the world for its healing long before I came on the scene. When I pray I simply enter into this ongoing stream, and my act of prayer, precious and important as it truly is, is swept up into something infinitely vaster and is cleansed for use.[6]

Thomas Merton developed a form of prayer based on insights he gleaned from the fourteenth-century *Cloud of Unknowing.* The object of this "centering prayer" approach is to go beyond words, thought, and images to simply be there. Thomas Keating, like Merton a Trappist monk, has said, "All you have to do is show up."[7] Basil Pennington, O.C.S.O., however, recommends the use of what he calls a "love word" or "prayer word" such as Jesus, *agape,* or the like as a kind of mantra. Begin by repeating the chosen word. If something distracts you during the time of meditation, draw yourself back by saying the "love word" again.[8] To remain centered, spend about twenty minutes twice a day in such focusing.

---

[6] Douglas V. Steere, *Traveling In,* ed. E. Glenn Hinson, Pendle Hill Pamphlets 324 (Wallingford, Pa.: Pendle Hill Publications, 1995), 18-19.

[7] Personal statement in a lecture. He has described the method in *Intimacy with God* (New York: Crossroad, 1994).

[8] M. Basil Pennington, O.C.S.O., *Centering Prayer: Renewing an Ancient*

I have reported several approaches to the daily retreat because there is no universally "right" one. Recognizing the centrality of this relationship with God, you will have to discover what works best for you. What you are looking for, I think, is what Douglas Steere has called "a frame of meaning,"[9] which will lift your work to a higher level and make you feel that what you are doing matters.

Weekly, Monthly, and Longer Retreats

In addition to these daily retreats, sustenance of the spiritual life in ministry to others will require longer periods of withdrawal for re-creation and re-collection of inner resources. Although most ministers take a day off each week, all too few make it "time to spare for God." Minimally, that would mean getting away at least once a month to spend an entire day in solitude. Perhaps more realistically, it should take place every week. A small ecumenical group of ministers in the Raleigh, North Carolina, area observe what they call "Sabbath time" every week. They spend seven hours every Wednesday, as one of the group describes it, "just wasting time."[10]

If you work under the kind of stress that Christian leaders regularly experience, you will also want to have longer retreats of at least thirty-six to forty-eight hours. Where would you go for such retreats? In this ecumenical era you are blessed with an abundance of splendid places of solitude and prayer because of the opening of Roman Catholic religious

---

Christian Form (Garden City, N.Y.: Doubleday Image Books, 1980), 65; *Call to the Center* (Hyde Park, N.Y.: New City Press, 1995), 13.

[9] Douglas V. Steere, *Work and Contemplation* (New York: Harper & Brothers, 1957).

[10] Mahan Siler, pastor of Pullen Memorial Baptist Church, Raleigh, N.C., in an unpublished address.

communities to non-Catholics. Even more traditionally enclosed communities such as the Abbey of Gethsemani near Bardstown, Kentucky, have refurbished their property in order to accommodate retreatants. These communities go about their central business of engaging in prayer and worship and establish a rhythm for the retreatants' time there. This time spent apart can help break the tyrannical pattern of an overcrowded calendar by which you may feel overextended and pressured.

Protestants have also established a significant number of retreat centers that are furnishing more and more of the things required for a genuinely re-creative retreat. Leading the way in this were Pendle Hill, founded in 1930 as a Quaker center for renewal and quickening of the spiritual life in Wallingford, Pennsylvania, and Kirkridge, a center founded near Harrisburg, Pennsylvania, in 1948 by John Oliver Nelson on the pattern of the Iona Community in Scotland.

The ecumenical wave that Pope John XXIII set in motion has had wonderful side effects. In Richmond, Virginia, for instance, an ecumenical center established specifically to pray for the city took over property vacated by the Sisters of Visitation, a religious order founded by Francis de Sales and Jane de Chantal in the seventeenth century. In the very heart of Richmond, churches, church staffs, and members have an ecumenical community gathering three times a day for prayer. Richmond Hill has developed a variety of programs, including RUAH, a training program in spiritual direction. A few years ago, Benedictine nuns in Madison, Wisconsin, let their convent become an ecumenical center involving both individuals and families.

A few congregations with substantial resources have developed retreat facilities useful not only for their members but for others. For example, Vienna Baptist Church in northern Virginia has established a center that will accommodate up to sixty-five persons on the edge of the George Washington

National Forest. Getting away from the scene of ministry so that you will not be tempted to rush back to pick up the work offers many advantages, but the most important is solitude. Be sure the place of retreat you select offers real solitude.

What do you do to make the most of the time of solitude? The answer to that is: The less you *do*, the more you will get out of the retreat. Remember, you are there to "spare some time for God," not to see how much you can get done! The single most important component of your retreat should be *silence*. One dimension of that is what the solitude automatically provides, that is, to take you physically away from the distractions that jangle your nerves and sap your energies. But that is only a part of what needs to happen. More important is that you become inwardly calm, tranquil, as Thomas Kelly puts it, "in childlike trust listening ever to Eternity's whisper, walking with a smile into the dark."[11]

On a retreat you will probably want to take your Bible, but do not take a boxful of other books to read. In most retreat centers you will find a good selection of devotional writings. But I do not even recommend that you do a lot of reading. A reading program all too easily perpetuates the busyness and distractedness that you are trying to overcome. Better to take your *journal*, and let it help you deepen your conversation with God.

If the retreat is a guided one, the retreat leader may set times for silence and meditation. Adapting a retreat model developed by Douglas Steere, I try to keep talk to a minimum. A good rule to follow comes from the Benedictines: "Speak only if it improves the silence." That cuts out a lot of babble. Forty-eight-hour retreats that I have conducted for students at Richmond Hill and in various other settings have had the following pattern:

---

[11] Thomas R. Kelly, *A Testament of Devotion* (New York: Harper & Brothers, 1941), 74

Theme: Contemplative Lifestyle

Friday

5:00 P.M.	Gathering and check in
6:00	Prayer with the community
6:30	Dinner
7:30	Presentation 1: "Prayer and Our Transformation" (Phil. 1:9-11)
8:15	Silence for meditation and journaling
9:30	Fellowship
11:00	Silence until morning prayer

Saturday

6:30 A.M.	Arise (in silence)
7:00	Morning prayer with the community
7:30	Breakfast
9:00	Presentation 2: "Making All of Life a Prayer" (1 Thess. 5:17)
9:45	Silence for meditation and journaling
10:15	Discussion in small groups
12:00 noon	Noon prayer
12:30 P.M.	Lunch
1:30	Rest, recreation, or silence
3:30	Presentation 3: "Prayer and Anxiety" (Phil. 4:5-7)
4:15	Silence for meditation and journaling
5:15	Discussion in small groups
6:00	Evening prayer
6:30	Dinner
7:30	Presentation 4: "Prayer and the Will of God" (Phil. 2:12-13)
8:15	Silence for meditation and journaling
9:30	Fellowship
11:00	Silence until morning prayer

Sunday

6:30 A.M.	Arise (in silence)
7:00	Morning prayer
7:30	Breakfast
9:00	Presentation 5: "Prayer and the Simplification of Life" (Matt. 6:33)
9:45	Silence for meditation and journaling
11:00	Worship with the community
12:00 noon	Lunch
1:00 p.m.	Departure

Some items in this schedule should be highlighted. (1) Notice that the theme holds the retreat together, but some may wish to follow their own paths as well. (2) Much time is scheduled for silence. Some may wish to have a totally silent retreat. Silence will maximize attentiveness to God's presence and love pouring on us or welling up within us. That attentiveness will open the way to renewal, restoration, and revitalization. (3) Even with and perhaps especially because of the silence, retreatants need some opportunity to share what is going on with them, whether in a small or large group or in individual conversation with the retreat leader. To permit a group to gain the most from the silence, retreat leaders can make themselves available for private conferences. Indeed, Douglas Steere *scheduled* individual conferences with each retreatant. (4) A community with an established prayer life offers a frame and establishes a rhythm for the retreat. If a group meets in a setting where the staff provide only physical comforts and support, the group needs to arrange its own corporate worship. Healthy spirituality depends on a balance of experiential, intellectual, social, and institutional. (5) Some retreat leaders read selections from the classics during meals, a Benedictine and Cistercian monastic practice, but silence may facilitate the re-creative process more than mental exercises. (6) Recognize the corporate dimension of spiritual growth, and schedule some time for fellowship. Sometimes these relaxing times open the way to very profound conversations that can have a life-changing impact.

Individual retreatants who will not have the structure suggested here would benefit from meeting with a spiritual director to reflect on what is taking place. Religious communities will usually make someone available if direction is requested.

Sabbaticals

People who exercise their callings in occupations as demanding as clergy need regular sabbaticals ranging from three months to a year no less than professors in colleges, universities, or seminaries. Recently, a friend and former student wrote and asked my advice. He has served as an editor of the denominational press and subsequently as pastor of two thriving congregations. He has had an exceptionally fulfilling ministry in the church of which he is currently pastor. The church has experienced significant increases in membership and giving. It has moved toward greater clarity about its relationship to the Southern Baptist Convention. The congregation has also undertaken a major building program. Meanwhile, my friend has carried weighty responsibilities in the state convention. These responsibilities have often brought him into conflict with other leaders. The cost of all of this is beginning to cause burnout. He wanted to know what to do.

My counsel was very pointed: Ask your church for a sabbatical. A short time later, he wrote to tell me that he had spoken to the personnel committee. They had also noticed the signs of burnout and were eager to encourage such a time. The sad reality is that many clergy grind on their starters so long that church members think they have reached a point of no return. Instead of thinking of the possibilities for renewal offered by a pastoral sabbatical, congregations may demand resignations or even fire a pastor. It is incredible how many immensely able ministers suffer such terminations. Churches desperately need to build in regular sabbaticals for staff members, and staff members need to insist on such times of spiritual care.

Because sabbaticals were connected with college or university faculty, you may have thought of sabbaticals as study leaves. Clergy may well need those, but today there is a far greater need to experience what the word sabbatical itself suggests: rest. You need to relax, take hands off for a while, and give yourself time for spiritual regeneration. You need to get in touch with the working of grace in your life. That is the real issue.

Where and how might you do that? When Henri Nouwen was teaching at Yale, he spent seven months at the Genesee Abbey near Rochester, New York. As a Roman Catholic, he probably felt free to explore whether he might have a calling to the contemplative life, but he did not experience such a call. However, something very significant did happen during the time there; he experienced a deep inward confirmation of God's love for him that he could carry back to Yale and other places he went subsequently.[12] Some ministers have been rewarded for having similar Sabbath rests.

Another former student asked me to serve as a sort of "spiritual guide" and mentor during a recent sabbatical that the congregation encouraged him to take. He, too, has had a very successful and fulfilling ministry. Church members hold him in highest esteem and affection. But he recognized his deep need for recharging his batteries. We discussed at length what he would do with this gift of time. One family in his congregation

---

[12]   Henri J. M. Nouwen, *The Genesee Diary: Report from a Trappist Monastery* (Garden City, N.Y.: Doubleday, 1976).

made a lovely cottage in the Blue Ridge Mountains available to him for the entire time, and he decided to make that his hermitage. Together we worked out a reading program in spirituality and worship. Each Sunday he worshiped with a different congregation so that he might experience worship of various Christian traditions. He spent a week in Washington, D.C., getting acquainted with the vibrant life of the Church of the Savior and another week in Holy Cross Abbey, a Trappist monastery near Berryville, Virginia. We met monthly to share what he was reading and what was happening both in his inner life and in his understanding of his calling. When he returned to his congregation, he went with renewed energy, expanded insight, and revitalized sense of calling. He had had a genuine sabbatical.

There is no single pattern for sabbaticals. You will do well to shape the experience to your specific circumstances. Some ministers have benefited from travel sabbaticals in which they could experience community in a variety of settings. A pastor friend who has operated under a lot of stress, for example, spent his six-month sabbatical in England and Israel. He engaged primarily not in study but in a restful time visiting historic sites. Most important for him was the opportunity to distance himself. Others have spent sabbaticals in programs for spiritual growth and direction such as Shalem offers in Washington, D.C. Others have lived in religious communities and taken part in all of the regular routine. One of my students spent the summer at the Abbey of Gethsemani, sharing the *Opus Dei*, the *lectio*, and the hours of manual labor just as the monks did. He even attended a chapter meeting. The possibilities for sabbatical are as limitless as your experience of God's love and mercy.

Chapter 10

SUSTAINING THE SPIRITUAL LIFE, III:
SHARING THE JOURNEY

Sustaining yourself in ministry will depend not only on attentiveness to God and times of withdrawal from the press and struggle but also on spiritual friendship and companionship. Ministry is often a long loneliness in which you cannot rest the burdens that you help others to carry. You hear highly personal and privileged confessions and assertions. You become a sharer of deep and painful injuries and hurts. You are made an observer of wanton wickedness and serious sin and the guilt attendant on them. You watch the health and life of earthly angels stealthily slip away and stare death in the face. You are present when all hell breaks loose in the homes of those you love. In such times you are desperate to find soul friends who, if nothing else, will listen to your cries of helplessness and rage and will remind you that "neither death, nor life, nor angels, nor rulers, nor things present, nor things to come, nor powers, nor height, nor depth, nor anything else in all creation, will be able to separate us from the love of God in Christ Jesus our Lord" (Rom. 8:38-39). Yes, even in less traumatic and more tranquil times, you can use some friends who can remind you that God is the first Guide of souls and that you are expendable and can lay down a lot of the burden that tries to crush you.

Spiritual friendship or companionship may take several forms. You may want and need one-on-one spiritual guidance by someone who can help you get in touch with the working of grace in your life. The Roman Catholic Church has required this for persons in religious orders and priests. Through the centuries the practice of oral confession has supplied ordinary believers with a modicum of spiritual guidance. In recent years not only Roman Catholics, Orthodox, or Anglicans but many Protestants have become interested in one-on-one spiritual direction or guidance. Individual guidance of this sort may not be available for you, however. You may feel more comfortable with group spiritual guidance or participation in a group of fellow strugglers. A group may diminish some of the intimate openness that one-on-one direction can assure, but it can supply stimulus to sharing that individual guidance may not. Much will depend on the buildup of trust both in individual and in group dynamics.

What Is Spiritual Guidance?

For a Christian leader who is sensitive to the need for a more formal kind of spiritual friendship, it will be useful to define what I mean by spiritual guidance and distinguish it from psychology, psychotherapy, or counseling. Monastic usage has favored the terms spiritual direction, but that idea sounds too authoritarian to many Protestants, especially in the Free Church tradition. Dietrich Bonhoeffer identified what lay behind this reserve in some lectures on *spiritual care* to seminarians at Finkenwalde: "Spiritual direction is a task of educating the populace carried out by the 'priest of the people.' In spiritual care, God wants to act. In the midst of all anxiety and sorrow we are to trust God. God alone can be a help and a comfort."[1] The Second Vatican Council has undermined much of the reason for the caution behind Bonhoeffer's words, but there is still some wisdom in using other terms that do not carry the baggage of the sixteenth century. Tilden Edwards has opted for spiritual friend,[2] Kenneth Leech for soul friend,[3] and Morton Kelsey for companions on the inner way.[4] Spiritual guide is also widely used.

Whether you continue to use the traditional spiritual direction or opt for one of the other designations, you must define how you understand the idea. Definition will obviously influence practice. Thomas Merton, speaking out of the Benedictine tradition, explains spiritual direction as "a continuous process of formation and guidance, in which a Christian is led and encouraged *in his [or her] special vocation*, so that by faithful correspondence to the graces of the Holy Spirit he [or she] may attain to the particular end of his [or her] vocation and to union with God."[5] Vocation is the key term here. By it Merton meant something broader than you may often understand. Vocation has to do with finding, under God, your special niche in life. In *Thoughts in Solitude* Merton wrote:

> A man [or woman] knows when he [or she] has found his [or her] vocation when he [or she] stops thinking about

---

[1] Dietrich Bonhoeffer, *Spiritual Care*, trans. Jay C. Rochelle (Philadelphia, Penn.: Fortress Press, 1982), 30.

[2] Tilden Edwards, *Spiritual Friend: Reclaiming the Gift of Spiritual Direction* (New York: Paulist Press, 1980).

[3] Kenneth Leech, *Soul Friend: The Practice of Christian Spirituality* (New York: Harper & Row, 1980).

[4] Morton T. Kelsey, *Companions on the Inner Way: The Art of Spiritual Guidance* (New York: Crossroad, 1983).

[5] Thomas Merton, *Spiritual Direction and Meditation* (Collegeville, Minn.: Liturgical Press, 1960), 5.

how to live and begins to live. . . .When we are not living up to our true vocation, thought deadens our life, or substitutes itself for life, or gives in to life so that our life drowns out our thinking and stifles the voice of conscience. When we find our vocation—thought and life are one.[6]

For most persons this vocational quest will continue throughout their lives. I'm not at all sure Merton ever got beyond where he was when he prayed:

My Lord God, I have no idea where I am going. I do not see the road ahead of me. I cannot know for certain where it will end. Nor do I really know myself, and the fact that I think I am following your will does not mean that I am actually doing so. But I believe that the desire to please you does in fact please you. And I hope I have that desire in all that I am doing. I hope that I will never do anything apart from that desire. And I know that if I do this you will lead me by the right road, though I may know nothing about it. Therefore I will trust you always though I may seem to be lost and in the shadow of death. I will not fear, for you are ever with me, and you will never leave me to face my perils alone.[7]

There are some other ways to think about spiritual guidance. Martin Thornton, an Anglican, defines spiritual guidance as "the positive nurture of [someone's] relation with God, the creative cultivation of *charismata*; the gifts and graces that all have received."[8] Eugene H. Peterson labels it "a

---

[6] Thomas Merton, *Thoughts in Solitude* (Garden City, N.Y.: Image Books, 1958), 85.

[7] Ibid., 81.

[8] Martin Thornton, *Spiritual Direction* (London: SPCK; Boston: Cowley, 1984), 10.

cultivated awareness that God has already seized the initiative."[9] Along similar lines, I think of spiritual guidance as helping others get in touch with the working of Grace, namely, God personally present, in their lives.

How does spiritual guidance differ from pastoral care, counseling, psychology, or psychotherapy? Actually, it is almost indistinguishable from *cura animae*, the designation early Christians used for pastoral care. Kenneth Leech wrote that spiritual guidance "is usually applied to the cure of souls when it involves the specific needs of the individual."[10] Numerous others use spiritual direction and the cure of souls synonymously. Most distinguish it decisively, however, from counseling, psychology, and psychotherapy.

Kenneth Leech noted three "crucial differences" between pastoral counseling and spiritual direction: (1) The pastoral counselor tends to focus on states of emotional distress, whereas spiritual direction "is a continuous ministry and involves the healthy as well as the sick."[11] (2) The counselor is clinic- or office-based, whereas the spiritual director "is firmly located within the liturgical and sacramental framework, within the common life of the Body of Christ."[12] (3) The counselor focuses on problems, the spiritual director on growth.[13] Merton underscored spiritual in spiritual direction and explained in this way:

> The whole purpose of spiritual direction is to penetrate beneath the surface of a [person's] life, to get behind the facade of conventional gestures and attitudes which he [or

---

9   Eugene H. Peterson, *The Contemplative Pastor: Returning to the Art of Spiritual Direction* (Dallas: Word, 1989), 69.
10 Leech, *Soul Friend*, 34.
11 Ibid., 100f.
12 Ibid., 101.
13 Ibid., 102.

she] presents to the world, and to bring out his [or her] inner spiritual freedom, his [or her] inmost truth, which is what we call the likeness of Christ in his [or her] soul. This is entirely a supernatural thing, for the work of rescuing the inner [person] from automatism belongs first of all to the Holy Spirit. The spiritual director cannot do such a work himself [or herself]. His [or her] function is to verify and to encourage what is truly *spiritual* in the soul.[14]

The key point is: God is the First Guide. You are an instrument. Always there is need for infinite patience. Sometimes you do well to get out of the way and let God work.[15]

Locating a Spiritual Friend

In this brief chapter I will not attempt to discuss a whole program of spiritual guidance, but it will be helpful to indicate some considerations as you try to locate a spiritual friend. Tilden Edwards has listed—not necessarily in order of importance— age, sex, experience, personality, spiritual path, faith tradition, and situation as major issues to keep in mind. Spiritual friend here refers to one-on-one guidance. One could, of course, belong to a group, but this discussion focuses on the pairing of friends.

Age is relative. What you really want to find in a spiritual guide is maturity, and that develops at different rates for different persons. Two issues, however, have prompted some to favor persons over forty-five as guides. By that time people usually pass the point where they are still striving to "make it" in life and where the competitive drive has slackened. In addition,

---

14 Merton, *Spiritual Direction and Meditation*, 8.
15 See E. Glenn Hinson, "Midwives and Mothers of Grace," *Theological Educator 63* (Spring 1991): 65-79.

the *libido* is supposed to diminish as people reach middle age. However, concern for these must not outweigh that for overall maturity.

Sex is an important consideration because you naturally relate to others as sexual beings. Here you will want to avoid a relationship that confuses and detracts from the main object: spiritual growth. Personal preference and experience will probably help you decide whether to choose a spiritual guide of the same or of the opposite sex. Much is to be said for operating on the principle of complementarity. If you are comfortable with it, a guide of the opposite sex might bring certain insights that someone of the same sex might miss. Men and women have long served as spiritual friends for each other.[16]

An adequate *experience* would include experience both of life and of God. You want a companion who has traveled far enough to know life and who has learned through the experience. A spiritual master has known pain and suffering as well as exhilarating moments and has reflected deeply. Inward processing should accompany external experience.

Personality type is also of relative significance. You are more likely to benefit from a guide whose personality complements rather than matches your own type, so long as the contrast is not so sharp that it interferes with understanding or leads to incompatibility. A person of moderately contrasting personality will hear and see things you may miss about yourself and raise questions you had not thought of.

The same principle applies to *spiritual path*. You will not gain the most from someone who is walking exactly the same path as you are. Edwards has identified four basic paths—devotion, action, knowledge (analytical or intuitive), and

---

[16] One of the most notable examples is that of Francis de Sales and Jane de Chantal, founders of the Sisters of Visitation.

"fighting it all the way."[17] Those on the devotional path are concerned with the beautiful, on the action path with the good, and on the knowledge path with the true. Those "fighting it all the way" are the skeptics. If you are on the devotional path, you might be challenged more by someone on the action, knowledge, or "fighting it all the way" path. If you are on the action path, by someone on the devotional, knowledge, or "fighting it all the way" path.

In a pluralistic society *faith tradition* may figure significantly in selection of a spiritual guide. You may feel comfortable only with someone of your own denomination, but that could be very limiting. If you have sunk your roots deeply in your own tradition, you may choose to reach across denominational lines and even outside Christianity. Much depends on whether the spiritual guide could understand and be appreciative of your faith and vice versa. That would be difficult if the faith traditions differed too much from each other.

Situation—professional minister, layperson, seminarian, or other—is another factor meriting consideration. A spiritual friend needs to have sufficient acquaintance with the role of guidee to clarify the vocation. A person in a position of authority, however worthy and well equipped personally, would not usually make a suitable guide because the position could constrict the openness essential to this friendship. Pastors, for instance, usually do not make good guides for subordinate staff whom they evaluate or professors for students whom they grade. Good spiritual direction, as Thomas Merton has pointed out, "implies an atmosphere of unhurried leisure, a friendly, sincere and informal conversation, on a basis of personal intimacy."[18] Relationships based on power do not often succeed.

In the final analysis, these considerations seem much

---

[17] Edwards, *Spiritual Friend*, 112-16. Compare the four dimensions of spirituality discussed in chapter 6.

[18] Merton, *Spiritual Direction and Meditation*, 25.

less important than certain qualities that you would want to find in a spiritual guide. The first and most important would seem to be the one cited first by Francis de Sales—*love*. The guide must be "full of charity."[19] *Agape*-love embodies the compassion that Julian of Norwich made the centerpiece of her guidance. God is, above all, a God of compassion, One who suffers with you and for you. God's compassion issues in Christ's passion. God stops at nothing, even human death, in order to demonstrate this love. A spiritual guide should try to imitate God.[20] From such love will come the capacity to be caring, sensitive, and accepting of others, factors essential in spiritual friendship.

A second quality is *knowledge*. This means more than book learning. Obviously, formal training is helpful, but it scarcely equals *experience*. The history, psychology, and theology of religious experience and spiritual direction will be beneficial. Yet equally if not more important is knowledge based on experience. In this case, as Richard Rolle chided the schoolmen of his day, it is still true that "a little old lady could be more experienced in love of God . . . than a theologian."[21]

Humility is another essential. The great spiritual masters have all underscored this. Unfortunately, the word humility is usually understood to signify a passive, dog-slinking attitude in the aggressive and often violent culture in which we live. The author of *The Cloud of Unknowing* viewed humility or meekness in a more positive way: "In itself, humility is nothing else but a [person's] true understanding and awareness of himself [or herself] as he [or she] really is." That based on two realities: human sin and weakness, on one side, and "the superabundant

---

[19] Francis de Sales, *Introduction to the Devout Life*, trans. Michael Day (London: J. M. Dent & Sons, 1961), 17.

[20] See Julia Gatta, *Three Spiritual Directors for Our Time* (Cambridge, Mass.: Cowley, 1987),

[21] Richard Rolle, *The Fire of Love and The Mending of Life*, trans. M. L. del Mastro (Garden City, N.Y.: Doubleday Image Books, 1981), 111.

love and worthiness of God," on the other[22]. Proper self-esteem is crucial in shaping other attitudes in spiritual guidance. Douglas Steere has pointed out that Baron Friedrich von Hüugel based his guidance on four premises: that God is "present and operative and laying siege to every soul before, during, and after any spiritual director might come upon the scene";[23] that he was himself "a needy one"; that "Souls are never dittos";[24] and that he "was himself expendable in the business of guiding souls."[25] Spiritual guides deliberately try to put themselves out of business, not to perpetuate a dependency. You should beware then, for you may feel called to spiritual guidance as a way of meeting personal needs and fostering long-term dependency. The object of the guidance, however, is to help another stand on his or her own feet.

Behind such qualities as these must stand *an active discipline of attentiveness to the First Guide* (prayer/meditation). It takes *discipline*, another difficult word in American culture. A multitude of things may squeeze out what most accounts for fruitful companionship. Good spiritual directors characteristically spend much time "leaning on the window sill of heaven."[26] As Claude Montefiore said on the death of von Hügel, "Souls like that, one has to have God to account for them."[27]

---

[22] *The Cloud of Unknowing*, ed. James Walsh, S.J., Classics of Western Spirituality (New York: Paulist Press, 1981), 148.
[23] Douglas V. Steere, ed., *Spiritual Counsel and Letters of Baron Friedrich von Hügel* (New York: Harper & Row, 1964), 10.
[24] Friedrich von Hügel, *Letters from Baron Friedrich von Hügel to a Niece*, ed. Gwendolen Greene (London: J. M. Dent & Sons, 1928), xxix.
[25] Steere, *Spiritual Counsel of von Hügel*, 12.
[26] The phrase was used by Douglas Steere, "*Journal*," 138, to describe the devotional regimen of Henry Hodgkin, a medical missionary to China and the first director of Pendle Hill.
[27] Cited by Douglas Steere, "*Journal*," 509.

Group Spiritual Friendship

One-on-one spiritual direction has been the norm in Roman Catholic religious orders and for priests. Such direction, despite its growth, will not become normative for Protestant religious leaders. For the most part, you will feel more at home with *groups* of fellow strugglers and pilgrims.

Spiritual friendship groups are amply attested in the history of Christianity. In the age of persecution through Constantine's conversion, house churches were close-knit families who encouraged, exhorted, and entreated one another. The little band who gathered around Augustine at Cassiciacum, an estate outside Milan, functioned in that way. One of that group, Nebridius, had left home and family in Carthage for no other reason than to accompany Augustine "in a most ardent search for truth and wisdom."[28] The group worked diligently to bring Augustine forth from the womb he had threshed around in for so long. Augustine paid them a high compliment: "In truth, I loved these friends for their own sakes, and I know that they in turn loved me for my own sake."[29] In the thirteenth century the Beguines gathered in small cell groups to pray, have Bible study, offer mutual support, and do deeds of love and kindness.[30] Judging by the poems of Hadewijch, the intimacy they sought occasioned pain as well as joy. In one long poem she lamented,

> They who early
> Catch sight of Love's beauty,

---

[28] *The Confessions of Augustine*, trans. John K. Ryan (Garden City, N.Y.: Image Books, 1960), 148.

[29] Ibid., 155.

[30] On the Beguines' customs see J. Van Mierle, S.J., "Beguins, Beguines, Beguinages," in *Dictionnaire de Spiritualite, Ascetique et Mystique* (Paris: Beauchesne, 1937), I:1341-52.

And are quickly acquainted with her joy,
And take delight in it—
If things turn out well for them,
Will have, God knows,
A much better bargain in love
Than I have found so far. [31]

The Friends of God and Brothers of the Common Life formed intimate communities like this too.[32] Philip Jacob Spener made earnest Bible study in small cell groups, like "the ancient and apostolic kind of church meetings" described by Paul in 1 Corinthians 14:26-40, the foundation for deliverance of the Lutheran churches from the hand of "deadening orthodoxy" in the seventeenth century.[33] John Wesley borrowed from the Moravians the cell-group idea they inherited from Pietism.

What is the nature of such spiritual friendship groups, and how are they formed? Most groups that I know have come into being out of a recognized need of persons for some unthreatening and affirming place to share what is going on in their lives. Usually one person has dropped a hint to one or two others who have had the same concern churning around inside, and they agree to explore possibilities, times and places to meet, and so forth.

What forms is perhaps most accurately described as a "covenant group." Members covenant with one another regarding the nature of the group and what they most want it to be. Essential to all such groups, however, would be acceptance, openness, caring, sensitivity, and capacity to listen. Covenant Groups in the Academy for Spiritual Formation sponsored by

---

[31] Hadewijch: *The Complete Works*, trans. Mother Columba Hart, O.S.B. (New York: Paulist Press, 1980), 152.

[32] Cf. R. R. Post, *The Modern Devotion* (Leiden: E. J. Brill, 1968), 353-58.

[33] Philip Jacob Spener, *Pia Desideria*, trans. and ed. Theodore G. Tappert (Philadelphia: Fortress Press, 1964), 89.

The Upper Room provide "an arena for deepening relationships" and "an opportunity to experience mutual spiritual guidance." Participants reflect together on shared experiences in a contemplative way. "Through listening and interaction, [they] can discover, affirm, and encourage the diversity of gifts within their group" and "help each other become aware of their own journeys and nurture and challenge each other to remain true to that journey."[34]

Acceptance, as Douglas Steere has said,[35] does not mean "toleration born of indifference." Rather, it would come very close to what *agape*-love signifies in the New Testament: embracing other persons without trying to shape them in your own mold. Community, genuine *koinonia*, depends on mutuality and respect for diversity. A group like this could well operate under the rubric Paul urged upon the Corinthians: "To each is given the manifestation of the Spirit for the common good" (1 Cor. 12:7).

If acceptance is authentic, it will assure *openness*. Openness to others does not mean that you will have no opinions. Quite to the contrary, persons who are most appreciative of the views of others will be those who feel secure in their own and can handle the give-and-take that will make a spiritual friendship group worthwhile. Openness is essential to frank and honest sharing. Members must be able to "let their hair down," as it were.

Caring is the heart of spiritual friendship. It pumps blood into acceptance and openness and causes them to grow. Baron von Hügel, speaking of spiritual direction, has remarked, "Caring is the best thing in the world; caring is all that matters; Christianity taught us to care."[36] As the bond of people in the

---

34 Danny E. Morris, "Birthing an Academy," The Upper Room, p. 6.

35 Douglas V. Steere, *On Listening to Another* (New York: Harper & Brothers, 1955), 12.

36 Quoted by Douglas V. Steere, "*Autobiography*, 1984," 3.

group grows stronger, the covenant group can become a kind of intercessory chain. The more open and deeper the sharing, the more it becomes a form of prayer in which the members lift one another up to God in joy and in sorrow, in faith and in doubt, in love and in anger. Sharers hold nothing in reserve because they know they can trust these friends with whom their lives are interknitted.

Conveners play a very important role in covenant groups in supplying leadership and fostering hospitality. Regarding leadership, Danny Morris has suggested that conveners use two types of questions to help members focus on their faith-sharing:

> 1. What is God saying to me today? What is the invitation? How is God inviting me? Calling me? What happened today that stirred something in me? How did it impact my life?
> 2. Where are my blocks? What gets in the way of my responding to God?

To assist in framing a group focus, conveners can ask:

> 1. Are we resolving conflict here, or are we avoiding conflict? What blocks do we need to let go of to be more open to each other?
> 2. How are we doing as a group?

Conveners are also responsible for hospitality. Hospitality is especially important to the covenant group. Participants need an environment that makes them feel comfortable and relaxes them. If they are to share openly, they will need a sense of community, a *koinonia*, they can trust. In *The Different Drum* M. Scott Peck has listed "the most salient characteristics of a true community": (1) inclusivity, commitment, and consensus, (2) realism, (3) contemplation, (4) a safe place, (5) a laboratory for personal disarmament, (6) a group that can fight gracefully, (7) a group of all leaders, (8) a spirit of peace.[37] These features are integrally interrelated. Exclusivism kills community. Inclusivity requires a commitment to coexist and to arrive at decisions through consensus. Reaching a commonly agreed decision demands realistic facing of the issues and a certain humility. Realism and humility grow out of a contemplative, self-scrutinizing approach. A true community creates an environment in which its members feel safe enough to cry in public, let down all of their defenses, and fight gracefully. After getting things started, the convener can turn the reins of leadership over to the whole group. As Peck has observed, it is more accurate to think of this not as a "leaderless" group but as "a group of all leaders."[38] What accounts for community of this sort is a spirit not of collective triumph but, as Thomas Kelly has said, "an eye-to-eye relationship of love which binds together those who live in the Center."[39]

Ecumenical Community

In bringing this chapter to a close, it seems worthwhile to remind you that you will find critical support and sustenance in the Body of Christ extending outward from local congregations to the ends of the earth. Luther spoke truly when he reminded his barber that, as he prayed, he did not pray alone. "Never think that you are kneeling or standing alone," he urged, "rather think that the whole of Christendom, all devout Christians, are standing there beside you and you are standing

---

[37] M. Scott Peck, *The Different Drum: Community-Making and Peace* (New York: Simon and Schuster, 1987), 59-76.

[38] Ibid., 72.

[39] Thomas R. Kelly, *A Testament of Devotion* (New York: Harper & Row, 1941), 78.

among them in a common, united petition which God cannot disdain."[40]

Every Christian leader should offer unending thanks to God for the incalculable change in ecumenical outlook wrought by Pope John XXIII and the Second Vatican Council. Today the pain of one (person, congregation, nation) is increasingly the pain of all, just as the joy of one is the joy of all. When you find yourself harassed and beleaguered and under siege, the first words of assurance and comfort are likely to come from outside your denomination and sometimes even from outside your faith tradition. The world Christian community now observes a Week of Prayer for Christian Unity that seems increasingly to become a week of prayer for one another. May you pay heed to the whole Body and to each member of the Body of Christ.

---

[40] Martin Luther, *A Simple Way to Pray*, in *Luther's Works* (Philadelphia, Penn.: Fortress Press), 43, 198.

Chapter 11

WHAT THE WORLD AND THE CHURCH NEED MOST

Many Protestants will be surprised to hear me say that what the world and the church need most are saints. Protestants have expended a lot of energy negating the whole idea of "holy persons" after whom we should model our lives. Scholars have pointed out that when Paul spoke about saints (*hagioi*), he referred to all Christians and not a select few. Like the Reformers, most Protestants have pooh-poohed the idea of an elite company of the committed who can serve as examples for the rest of us.

I am not calling for a return to the cult of saints, relics, prayers to and for the saints, and all the other paraphernalia of piety that led to such great abuses in the Middle Ages. I am interested, rather, in living saints—such as Anna in Luke 2:36-38, who, as a widow, "never left the temple but worshiped there with fasting and prayer night and day." Or Perpetua, the young Carthaginian who, while still a catechumen, gave her life for her faith in the persecution under the Emperor Septimius Severus about 203.[1]   Or Augustine (354–430), who, once he yielded himself fully to God, became the Latin world's most influential theologian. Or Julian of Norwich (1343–ca. 1416), whose experience of God as a God of infinite compassion made her one of the most sought after spiritual guides of her day. Or Martin Luther (1483–1546), stalwart reformer who stood fast in the face of threats of emperors and popes. Or, in more recent centuries, John Woolman (1720–72), who, from age twenty-six until his death of smallpox in England, spent about one month out of every year traveling the American colonies to plead with Quakers to free their slaves. Or Martin Luther King Jr. (1929–68), a Gandhi imitator who at age twenty-seven was drafted to lead the nonviolent movement for civil rights in the United States. Or Clarence Jordan (1912–69), New Testament scholar, founder of Koinonia Farm, and inspirer of Habitat for Humanity and Jubilee Partners, a refugee ministry.

What Is a Saint?

A saint is not a perfect person, someone who never makes a mistake. Indeed, saints often make the most embarrassing mistakes that may lead to their being dropped from the list of saints like hot potatoes. Many, for instance, would strike Martin Luther King Jr.'s name from the roll because of certain liaisons with women connected with the civil rights movement.[2]   Thomas Merton may never make it through the beatification and canonization process of the Catholic

---

[1]   *The Martyrdom of Saints Perpetua and Felicitas* includes her "*Diary*," the first identifiable writing by a woman.

[2]   Kentucky's first African-American woman senator, Georgia Davis Powers, has claimed sexual liaisons involving M. L. King Jr. in a book entitled *I Shared the Dream* (Far Hills, N.J.: New Horizon Press, 1995), 145-62, 169-77, 179-86, 227-35.

Church as a consequence of the romance he had with a nurse in a Louisville hospital a short while before he died. Saints are not perfect.

Saints are not extraordinary, either. "I knew nothing; I was nothing," one saint said about herself. "For this reason God picked me out."[3] The world does not have many geniuses, but it can have many saints, for the life of a saint is open to all, even geniuses. What is required for a genius to become a saint is the same thing that is required of everyone, yielding to God. What matters is what God does with the capacities that people give over to God's use. As Douglas Steere has pointed out in a lecture "The Authority of the Saint," saints come in highly diversified personalities—

a vacillating Peter; a mystically-minded John; an authoritarian Jewish law-giver, Paul; strong, passionate, willful dispositions like those of Tertullian, Augustine, and Pascal; eclectic, balanced, rational natures like Clement of Alexandria, and Origen, Aquinas and Erasmus; poets and minnesingers like Francis of Assisi and Jacopone da Todi, Henry Suso, Thomas Traherne and Francis Thompson; difficult personalities with naturally fragile and often disrupted psycho-physical dispositions, such as those of Catherine of Genoa, Teresa of Avilá, or Søren Kierkegaard; a mother of many children and an eminently practical administrator like Bridget of Sweden; a German cobbler, Boehme; an English leatherworker, Fox; a New Jersey tailor, Woolman; an illiterate French peasant who could not pass his theological examinations and was so particularly deficient in moral theology that it was thought wise for years not to trust him to hear confessions, the Curé of Ars.[4]

---

[3] Catherine Laboure cited by Jill Haak Adels, *The Wisdom of the Saints: An Anthology* (New York: Oxford University Press, 1987), 130.

[4] Douglas V. Steere, *On Beginning from Within* (New York: Harper Brothers, 1943), 43.

What, then, is a saint? In his inaugural lecture as the Harry Emerson Fosdick Visiting Professor at Union Theological Seminary in New York in 1961, Douglas Steere listed six qualities.[5] Saints, first of all, are *persons whose lives have been irradiated by Divine Grace and have put themselves at God's disposal.* They are those who have discovered the Real and, ever after, must be answerable to what is real. Like Dag Hammarskjöld, brilliant and dedicated secretary general of the United Nations, they have said yes to Something or Someone. "God does not die on the day when we cease to believe in a personal deity," he wrote in his journal, "but we die on the day when our lives cease to be illumined by the steady radiance, renewed daily, of a wonder, the source of which is beyond all reason."[6]

As persons whose lives have been infused with Grace, second, *saints seek not to be safe but to be faithful.* "They never seem to be spared from troubles, but only to look at trouble through different eyes," Douglas Steere has said.[7] When reporters interviewed Mother Teresa of Calcutta, they frequently asked how she and her Sisters of Charity could go on picking up nearly lifeless bodies from the streets when they rarely see one survive. She responded, "God did not call me to be successful. God called me to be faithful." She called herself "God's pencil."[8] What was her perspective?

---

[5] He gave a slightly different list in *On Beginning from Within*, 9-28: (1) saints begin from within, with referring the smallest action to God; (2) they manifest "a simple unassuming heroism that stops at nothing when his [her] witness to his [her] dearest love is at stake"; (3) they possess "staying power" or "gristle"; (4) they practice personal care for others; (5) they do not separate sacred and secular but consider all life sacramental; and (6) yet they are fallible.

[6] Dag Hammarskjöld, *Markings*, trans. Leif Sjöberg and W. H. Auden (London: Faber and Faber, 1964), 64.

[7] Douglas V. Steere, "Spiritual Renewal in Our Time," *Union Seminary Quarterly Review* 17 (November 1961): 47.

[8] Mother Teresa, *My Life for the Poor*, ed. José Luis González-Balado and Janet N. Playfoot (San Francisco, Harper & Row, 1985), 95.

I never look at the masses as my responsibility. I look only at the individual. I can love only one person at a time. I can feed only one person at a time.

Just one, one, one.

You get closer to Christ by coming closer to each other. As Jesus said, "Whatever you do to the least of my brethren, you do it to me."

So you begin . . . I begin.

I picked up one person—maybe if I didn't pick up that one person I wouldn't have picked up all the others.

The whole work is only a drop in the ocean. But if we don't put the drop in, the ocean would be one drop less.

Same thing for you. Same thing in your family. Same thing in the church where you go. Just being . . . one, one, one.[9]

Saints receive no exemption from trouble. To the contrary, as William Russell Maltby insisted, Jesus promised his followers only that they should be "absurdly happy, entirely fearless, and always in trouble."[10] Given this kind of promise, saints, third, are *those who have learned how to get along in adversity*. They have developed stick-to-itiveness. Like the collection of social and personal misfits whom Dorothy Day and Peter Maurin attracted to the Catholic Worker movement during the depth of the Great Depression in 1932, they "get along somehow."[11]

Saints, fourth, are *joyful*. The Apostle Paul ranked it just after love as a "fruit of the Spirit" (Gal. 5:22-23). God's will in

---

[9] Michael Collopy, *Works of Love Are Works of Peace: Mother Teresa and the Missionaries of Charity* (San Francisco: Ignatius Press, 1996), 35.

[10] Cited by Steere, "Spiritual Renewal in Our Time," 48.

[11] Ibid., 50. On Dorothy Day and the Catholic Worker movement see William D. Miller, *Dorothy Day: A Biography* (San Francisco: Harper & Row, 1982), 249-80.

Christ is that we "rejoice always, pray without ceasing, give thanks in all circumstances" (1 Thess. 5:16-18). He rejoiced, his imprisonment and approaching death notwithstanding (Phil. 1:18-19). The Philippians, too, should rejoice always. Sensing their puzzled expressions, he repeated, "Again I will say, Rejoice. Let your gentleness be known to everyone" (Phil. 4:4-5). Saints rejoice not *because* of what is happening but because "the Lord is near." Thus could Francis of Assisi find "unspeakable joy" in sufferings on behalf of Christ to the point that some thought him a little loony. For, Francis judged, "the devil rejoices most when he can snatch away spiritual joy from the servant of God. He carries dust so that he can throw it into even the tiniest chinks of conscience and soil the candor of mind and purity of life. But when spiritual joy fills hearts, the serpent throws off his deadly poison in vain."[12] Teresa of Avila prayed that she might be "delivered from sour, vinegary Christians."[13] Those dour Puritans in New England made a big mistake. They seemed fearful that some might be enjoying themselves. Saints are joy filled.

Saints, fifth, are *"kindlers and purifiers of the dream."*[14] Saints are dreamers. They have visions of what God is trying to bring into being. They pray, "Your kingdom come. Your will be done, on earth as it is in heaven" (Matt. 6:10). Not only do they have dreams; they try to act out their dreams. Like Albert Schweitzer, who relinquished a distinguished post as a theologian in Germany in order to train himself as a medical doctor and spend his life in Lambaréné. Or Arthur Shearly Cripps, who, inspired by the model of Francis of Assisi, turned aside from a promising future as a poet to spend the rest of his

---

[12] Thomas of Celano *Second Life* 125, in *Saint Francis of Assisi: Writings and Early Biographies*, trans. Raphael Brown et al., ed. Marion A. Habig (Chicago: Franciscan Herald Press, 1972), 465.

[13] Cited by Steere, "Spiritual Renewal in Our Time," 51.

[14] Ibid.

life among the Mashonas in Rhodesia, sharing to the full their deeply impoverished lives.[15] Saints "long to dare and are daring."[16]

Finally, and above all, saints are *prayerful*. They are those who constantly open themselves to the besieging love of God. Nothing so marks the life of the saint as the inner attention and yielding to God. The priest in Bernanos's classic novel The *Diary of a Country Priest* brings his life to a close with the prayer of a saint: "Dear God, I give all to You, willingly. But I don't know how to give, I just let You take. The best is to remain quiet. Because though I may not know how to give, You know how to take. . . . Yet I would have wished to be, once, just once, magnificently generous to You."[17]

Saints' Impact on Individual Lives

That, then, is what saints are: persons whose lives have been irradiated by Grace; seek not to be safe but to be faithful; get along in adversity; are joyful; are dream filled; and, above all, are prayerful. Can such persons make a difference in our world? Not many, I think, would dispute that saints can influence individual lives. One such saint etched himself on my life.

His name was O. C. Marsh, a name you will not know. His name appeared in a newspaper only when he died. Yet who I am is to a great degree a consequence of the impact of this ordinary, inconspicuous saint.

As a four-year-old I began to learn what grace is from

---

[15] On Cripps see Douglas V. Steere, *God's Irregular: Arthur Shearly Cripps* (London: SPCK, 1973).

[16] Steere, "Spiritual Renewal in Our Time," 53-54.

[17] Georges Bernanos, *The Diary of a Country Priest* (London: Carroll & Graf Publishers, Inc., 1994), 296-97.

him. My family were fishing in Brush Creek near Cuba, Missouri, which ran alongside his farm. I stood holding my pole until long after the minnows or little fish had nibbled all the worm off my hook. Uncle Osse noticed. He sidled over, got between me and my line, and lifted it up, saying, "Glenn, let's see what we've got here." He slipped a little perch onto my hook and dropped it back into the water. You can't imagine the joy of my first catch or my first touch of grace.

From him I learned what compassion is. When my mother and father divorced after a stormy marriage, my aunt and uncle took my older brother and reared him. A short time after that, they took two cousins and cared for them for four years when their mother had to enter a tuberculosis sanatorium.

From him I learned what humility is. My uncle was not a shy person, but he never put himself forward for anything, and he "awshucked" his way out of any honors or plaudits. By example he taught me that none of us is too special to do the most menial task. He was content to earn his living as a farmer and as a barber.

From him I learned how to distinguish between wisdom and knowledge. My uncle had only an eighth grade education, but he was one of the wisest persons I have ever known. He knew what mattered most in life—love, joy, peace, patience, kindness, goodness, faithfulness, meekness, self-control, the fruit of the Spirit (Gal. 5:22-23).

From him I learned what faithfulness means. When I attended Washington University in St. Louis, I lived with my aunt and uncle, who by then had moved from Cuba to St. Louis. I had not yet developed a practice of regular church attendance. Neither my aunt nor my uncle talked much about faith. They did not push their commitment at me, but they lived it. Their faith controlled their everyday lives. When the church was open, they went. When someone had a need, they gave. When someone was sick, they visited and they prayed. They never preached to me about going to church, but I found myself compelled by their example and was soon drawn deeply into the same life of faith. I hope this story connects with a story from the well of your memory.

Can Saints Make a Difference in Our World?

The harder question with which I began is whether saints can make a difference in the larger community and the world. Here many observers tend to be skeptical. "Sure, they can affect individual lives. Maybe even groups. But the larger world is another matter." Indeed, one theory of history assumes that individuals scarcely matter. We float like chips in a stream drifting wherever the current flows.

Saints deny this theory, but most of us can understand the skepticism. After all, saints are not primarily social reformers. Most people would think pretentious the tee shirts and posters students at the Southern Baptist Theological Seminary featured in the optimistic 1980s. They declared boldly, "We're out to change the world." Saints also are not professors putting before society an irresistible argument. As Douglas Steere has pointed out, they simply put before people their lives "and an embarrassing invitation which they must decide to accept or reject."[18] How, then, can they influence more than those few persons with whom they come in contact? Still more, how can one argue that saints are what the world and the church need most?

Douglas Steere argued in *On Beginning from Within* that saints, precisely in incarnating a dream, can affect society at its

---

[18] Steere, *On Beginning from Within*, 17.

"vulnerable center" and lift it to a new level of faithfulness.[19] The key lies in the saints' "own striking faithfulness to something that transcends society." He went on to say, "So long as staunch, devoted Christian individuals remain, there is at work in society a powerful force to reassert the principle of order and to compel the state or any social institution to consider its relation to the true end of individual men [and women]."[20]

Let me present my case with two lives interconnected with each other despite being more than seven centuries apart—Francis of Assisi (1182–1226) and Mother Teresa of Calcutta (1910–97). The link lies in the fact that Mother Teresa modeled her life after the example of Francis.

During his first twenty years, few could have suspected that Francis would turn out to be a saint who would leave an enduring mark on world history. Born into the affluent family headed by Peter Bernadone, the future saint paid scant attention to the homeless people who begged at Assisi's gates, the people with leprosy who had to live in an enclave outside the city, or those who took up the cross and went to war. He took full advantage of the benefits of affluence.

When he was about twenty, however, he took part in something that led to a dramatic turn in his life. The city of Assisi mounted a campaign against the neighboring city of Perugia, a very ill-advised decision, for Perugia was an impregnable fortress. Francis did not consider the wisdom of the action. Like other dutiful citizens of Assisi, he outfitted himself with horse, armor, and the other trappings of war and set out for Perugia. Before he reached his destination, he was captured and spent more than a year in prison before his wealthy father ransomed him.

Solitude, even forced solitude, often changes people. When Francis returned to Assisi, people noticed something

---

19 Ibid., 31.
20 Ibid., 30.

different about him. He spent more time alone. He was more serious, and he began to do peculiar things. We do not know the exact order in which these things occurred, but over a period of about five years Francis experienced a radical transformation. When a nobleman of Assisi mounted a campaign against Apulia, Francis, inspired by dreams of increased wealth and fame, consented to go, but first illness and then a vision caused him to offer the implements of war he had collected to another soldier.[21] Deciding to break through the uncertainty and confusion of his bellicose age by simply following Jesus as literally as he could, he sold cloth stolen from his father's shop and, as he phrased it, "married Lady Poverty."[22] He tried to give the money to a priest at St. Damian, a very run-down church, but the priest refused to accept it, fearing Francis's parents. Francis threw the money down on a windowsill.[23] Peter Bernardone, convinced that his son had lost his mind, caught up with Francis and locked him in the dark basement of his house (evidently to get him out of the beams of the moon [luna] that had led to his lunacy!). Francis's mother finally took pity on her son and let him go. His father, however, tracked Francis down and dragged him before the bishop to get him to turn all of his possessions over to himself. Francis promptly accommodated his father by stripping himself naked. He would have gone away without a stitch except that the bishop covered him with his mantle.[24]

This complete rupture with his family freed Francis for radical discipleship. Henceforth, he sought nothing so much as to follow Jesus, and to do that in all of its painful simplicity. He went to care for the lepers whom he could not stand the sight or stench of before, once even kissing a leper.[25] He repaired the

---

[21] Thomas of Celano *First Life* 4-5.

[22] Ibid., 6-7.

[23] Ibid., 8-9.

[24] Ibid., 10-15.

[25] Ibid., 17.

church of St. Damian and the Portiuncula, which he made headquarters for his little band of followers.[26] He set out, according to Jesus' directives, to preach a message of peace and, when others joined him, sent them out two by two to do the same. He instructed them: "Go, my dearest brothers, two by two into the various parts of the world, announcing to men peace and repentance unto the forgiveness of sins."[27] In these small and inconspicuous efforts lay the germ of a powerful idea that, in a century, would capture the imagination of Christians throughout Europe and start the movement that would bring the senseless Crusades to an end.

Francis came up with this daring thought at the height of the Crusades. In 1204 occurred the disastrous Fourth Crusade, in which the whole purpose of the Crusades took a radical turn. The Crusades were launched originally in 1095 in order to rescue the Byzantine (Eastern Christian) Empire from the Turkish threat. In the Fourth Crusade Venetian merchants persuaded crusaders to capture the trading city of Zara as the price of transportation to the Holy Land by ship. To take Zara, the crusaders had to capture Constantinople and thus reduce the Byzantine Empire to a tiny kingdom centered on Nicaea. In 1212 came the Children's Crusade. Children aged twelve to eighteen set out to do with childhood innocence what heavily armed knights had failed to do with the sword. Those who tried to march overland died en route of malnutrition, exposure to the elements, and marauders. Unscrupulous merchants carried others to Egypt by ship and sold them into slavery.

Francis, too, aspired to go to the Holy Land, as Bonaventure judged, "not to kill, but in hope of being killed."[28]

---

[26] Ibid., 18, 21.

[27] Ibid., 23-25, 29. Francis also incorporated the peace message into his *Canticle of Brother Sun*: "Happy those who endure in peace, By you, Most High, they will be crowned."

[28] Bonaventure *Major Life* 9.5.

He hoped by preaching and martyrdom to win others to Christ. In 1219, "the thirteenth year of his conversion," he set out for Syria and eventually reached Damietta in Egypt, where he was captured but released after he met with the sultan.[29] "Until this moment," John Holland Smith has written, "he had never known the limits of his courage: now he knew that he would dare anything for Christ."[30] He paid a terrible price for his pilgrimage. By the time he returned to Assisi his little band had been taken under wing by Cardinal Ugolino, the bishop of Ostia, and Francis himself soon became a humble lay brother in an order he did not intend to found.[31] More complex rules, one in 1221 and the other in 1223, replaced the simple one he had devised. His health broke down completely by 1226. He was nearly blind. He died October 4, 1226.

His was a short life, an inconspicuous life, but a life yielded to God and placed before others with an invitation to which they had to respond. Did that life have a world-changing impact? You judge. Later generations remembered him with wonderful stories. How he preached to the birds, who stretched their wings and stood on their tails to make the sign of the cross.[32] How he tamed a pack of fierce wolves at Greccio[33] and even the awful wolf of Gubbio.[34] How a little rabbit, when freed from a trap, fled to Francis and nestled in his bosom.[35] How he endured abuse, insult, and injury and forgave his tormentors.[36] True joy, he taught, is the Cross alone.[37] The

---

[29] Celano *First Life* 57.
[30] John Holland Smith, *Francis of Assisi* (New York: Charles Scribner's Sons, 1972), 132.
[31] Ibid., 75.
[32] Ibid., 58.
[33] Bonaventure *Major Life* 11; *Legend of Perugia* 34.
[34] *The Little Flowers of St. Francis*, 21.
[35] Celano *First Life* 60.
[36] Ibid., 16.
[37] *The Little Flowers of St. Francis*, 8.

image was one of peace, reconciliation with all nature and all humankind. Long after Francis had died, they put in his mouth the words of that wonderful prayer we call "The Prayer of Saint Francis":

> Lord, make me an instrument of thy peace:
> Where there is hatred, let me sow love;
> Where there is injury, pardon;
> Where there is doubt, faith;
> Where there is despair, hope;
> Where there is darkness, light;
> Where there is sadness, joy

> O, Divine Master, grant that I may not so much seek
> To be consoled as to console;
> To be understood as to understand;
> To be loved as to love;
> For it is in giving that we receive;
> It is in pardoning that we are pardoned;
> It is in dying that we are born to eternal life.

Did this represent accurately what Francis taught? It may not matter because this was what impressed people everywhere from then on, but it appears accurate. In a biography of Francis, John Holland Smith has cited Thomas of Spalato, who had heard Francis preach. Spalato said "that the key to his appeal was his unceasing emphasis on the importance of peace 'for indeed, everything he said was directed towards the extinction of enmity, and re-establishing the brotherhood of peace.'" Smith has added, "In preaching peace, he was speaking for, as well as to, the poor, to whom the constant words and threats of war of the times meant nothing but additional burdens in a life already all but intolerably hard."[38]

---

[38] Smith, *Francis of Assisi*, 164-65.

Francis's life mattered. The world has long since forgotten most of the mighty men of valor who went on the Crusades, but not Francis. His peace message ushered in a kinder and gentler Europe. It signaled the beginning of the end for the senseless Crusades. Francis's example has inspired peacemakers and movements ever since.

I could list many names of Francis's imitators in following Jesus, but for our own day one stands out: Mother Teresa of Calcutta. When she received the Nobel Prize for Peace in 1979, some protested. "This saintly nun's pronouncements are entirely devoid of any element of prophetic criticism," one person wrote soon afterward.[39] She was no Martin Luther King Jr. As a matter of fact, she was not a peace activist. Rather, like Francis of Assisi, she was simply a saint yielding her life to God in wholehearted service of the poor. That meant educating children, washing putrid sores of the dying, caring for lepers whom society shunned, taking in street urchins, giving medication to tuberculars, and in sum, loving the unwanted, unloved, and abandoned.

Before she became known as Mother Teresa, Agnes Gonxha Bojaxhiu was born in Skopje in what is now Macedonia in 1910. When she was twelve, she heard a Jesuit missionary speak about the desperate plight of the poor in India. There grew within her, little by little, a sense of calling. The Sisters of Loretto made it possible for her to go to India, and for nine years she taught in one of their schools. Seeing a corpse in the gutter one day, however, stirred within her a conviction that God wanted her to do something special—to minister to the poorest of the poor. She had trouble arranging a release from the Sisters of Loretto and obtaining the approval of the archbishop of Calcutta, but her perseverance paid off. So did her determination to do everything for Christ. "I am nothing. He is all. I do nothing

---

39 Jack A. Jennings, "A Reluctant Demurrer on Mother Teresa," *Christian Century*, March 11, 1981, 258.

on my own. He does it," she said. "That is what I am, God's pencil. A tiny bit of pencil with which he writes what he likes."[40]

Mother Teresa died in September 1997. At this point who can say for sure how the life and the invitation she put before us will mark humankind? I would venture the bold assertion that long after the world has forgotten the political and economic power brokers of today, it will remember Mother Teresa. Because she put before us a life of selfless love, she has made the world a kinder and gentler and more thoughtful place. "Love is not a word," she said on receiving the Bellarmine Medal in Louisville, Kentucky, on June 22, 1987. "Love is life. People are hungry for more than bread. They are hungry for love. Love is a gift of God. We must love with a pure heart."[41]

The church and the world need saints. They need saints more than they need more canny politicians, more brilliant scientists, more grossly overpaid executives and entrepreneurs, more clever entertainers and talk-show hosts. Are there any on the horizon now that Mother Teresa is no longer with us, either of the extraordinary or of the ordinary kind? I think there are. Maybe I should say that there are saints "aborning" by God's grace. There are those whose lives have been irradiated by God's grace, who seek not to be safe but to be faithful, who have learned how to get along in adversity, who are joyful, who are dream filled, and, above all, who are prayerful. That is what the church and the world need most. It begins with you.

---

40 Mother Teresa, *My Life for the Poor,* 95.
41 My personal recording of her talk.

Appendix

PERSONALITY AND SPIRITUALLY

You may wonder why you have difficulty maintaining certain disciplines, such as sitting in silence for even short periods of time or using certain forms of prayer. I could cite any number of reasons, but contemporary psychological studies indicate that personality type will enter prominently into the equation. Extroverts, for instance, will be likely to find silence and meditation a challenge, whereas introverts may take to silence like bees to goldenrods.

Let me underscore at the outset, however, that personality type does not make one person more or less spiritual or acceptable to God than another. Although some will find spiritual disciplines easier than others, that should not cause us to create categories such as the ancient Gnostics used: hylic ("material"), pneumatic ("spiritual"), and psychic (somewhere between the other two). The Gnostics considered the hylic spiritually hopeless, the pneumatic automatic entrants into heavenly realms, and the psychic strugglers in things spiritual. Modern instruments such as the Myers-Briggs Personality Inventory register preferences or inclinations related to personality type; they do not make judgments about the spiritual value of those preferences.

As you open yourself to God, you should recognize that God can enable you to transcend limitations that personality or life experiences or anything else may impose. If grace is greater than your sins (Rom. 5:15, 20), grace must also be greater than effects of personality. Charles J. Keating observed, "Our basic personality is a starting point, not a jail."[1] Many factors such as culture, economics, and past religious experience influence your spirituality. Openness and yieldedness to God matter most in the religious realm. You need not let a psychological profile control your life.

How Personality Types Affect Spirituality

Personality, however, does have an impact on preferences or inclinations toward certain types of prayer or approaches to spirituality. Although the major emphasis of this appendix will fall on pairing certain approaches to spirituality, you should give some attention to the "leanings" caused by differences in personality. As you reflect on these broad observations, you must not forget individual uniqueness. God deals with each person one by one by one and not by personality profile.

Carl Jung sorted out four pairs of personality types: Introvert-Extrovert, Intuitive-Sensing, Feeling-Thinking, and Perceiving-Judging. These pairs should be viewed as ranging across a spectrum. If you tend toward the extreme, you will want to engage in spiritual exercises that may pull you more toward the center. Spiritual growth requires stretching toward the weak

---

1 Charles J. Keating, *Who We Are Is How We Pray: Matching Personality and Spirituality* (Mystic, Conn.: Twenty-Third Publications, 1987), 118.

side in order to achieve greater balance. A general study of the pairs is not needed here, but it may be helpful to consider also the impact of the Myers-Briggs Personality Inventory on your understanding of spirituality.

The Myers-Briggs Inventory offers a number of statements to which responses are given based on one's preferences. These responses are scored and placed on a grid to show some of the general traits of an individual's personality. Note that personality type is different from behavior. For example, a person who shows a decided introvert personality may demonstrate the commonly understood traits of an extrovert; even so, that person will prefer and show the introvert personality on the inventory.

I do not have the space to go into the specific traits of the Myers-Briggs pairs. I hope that you will take the inventory if you have not and that you will also read some of the literature that examines the Myers-Briggs Inventory and spirituality. Charles J. Keating in one of those works has noted the impact of personality types as follows:

1. *Introverted* spirituality is "complex" and "non-conforming" and therefore "personal." *Extroverted* is no easier or simpler than introverted, but it is "more coherent" and "forthcoming" to others.

2. *Intuitives* are dreamers. Consequently, their spirituality makes much use of imagination. Intuitives are always projecting possibilities and exploring implications. Sensing types, on the other hand, want solid ground. They have a realistic view of the world around them. Interestingly, they constitute the majority of people who work in religious institutions. "Dreamers" may have trouble surviving in organizations that expect much of them.

3. *Feelers* want to accept responsibility for those around them. They think of God as their Coworker. They have difficulty with spiritual growth because they tend to undervalue it.

Thinkers, by contrast, value reason and logic and have trouble with spiritual growth because they question it.

4. *Judging* personalities are uncomfortable with ambiguity and want something they can control. In the religious realm this includes spirituality and God. They find it difficult to allow anyone, God included, to take over. *Perceivers*, on the other hand, are open and take what comes without a lot of fuss. They are risk takers.

Finding a Spirituality for Your Type

Through the centuries Christianity has produced a cornucopia of spiritualities that can be matched with different personality types. Although the many religious orders and denominations share some of the same basic features, each possesses certain distinctives that appeal to certain personality types. Thus far, most of the matching seems to have been done with Roman Catholic religious orders, but you can easily imagine the attraction exerted by certain Protestant or Orthodox traditions, each of which may represent certain spiritualities similar to Catholic religious orders. Methodists, for instance, have long been thought of as Protestant Franciscans. With their emphasis on silence Quakers share much with the Benedictine tradition.

Charles Keating has matched personality types with four types of Catholic spirituality—Ignatian, Salesian, Teresian, and Chardinian. His research connects the personality types with these approaches to Christian spirituality in a provocative way.

Chester P. Michael and Marie C. Norissey have matched prayer forms and personality types with somewhat different results. Looking at two rather than all four of the dominant traits, they have paired the Sensing-Judging temperament with the highly disciplined Ignatian method of prayer, which relies heavily on imagination. In the *Spiritual Exercises* Loyola gave a variety of suggestions about prayer. In addition to undertaking careful self-examination three times a day and meditating on the Gospels, he commended three other methods of prayer: (1) meditating on the Ten Commandments, the seven deadly sins, the three powers of the soul, and the five senses of the body; (2) considering the significance of each word of a prayer; and (3) rhythmically reciting the Lord's Prayer, Ave Maria, Anima Christi, Credo, and Salve Regina.

Intuitive-Feeling types may prefer an Augustinian approach. Whereas Ignatian prayer "projects" its users into the scene by "sensible imagination," Augustinian prayer "transposes" the words of scripture to the modern situation by "creative imagination."[2] The major concern is not to understand the words in their original context so much as to see what they mean now. The Apostle Paul had something like this in mind when he cited the example of Israel in the desert wanderings as a warning to the Corinthians. "These things happened to them to serve as an example," he said, "and they were written down to instruct us, on whom the ends of the ages have come" (1 Cor. 10:11). Cassian of Marseilles reported a similar method of the desert fathers and mothers in using the Psalms. According to Abba Isaac, we are to recite the Psalms in

> the same attitudes of heart wherein the Psalmist wrote or sang his psalms, we shall become like the authors....And when we use the words, we remember, by a kind of meditative association, our own circumstances and struggles, the results of our negligence or earnestness, the mercies of God's providence or the temptations of the

---

2   Chester P. Michael and Marie C. Norissey, *Prayer and Temperament: Different Prayer Forms for Different Personality Types* (Charlottesville, Va.: The Open Door, Inc., 1984), 58.

devil, the subtle and slippery sins of forgetfulness or human frailty or unthinking ignorance.[3]

The key would seem to be "meditative association." Although all persons of all temperaments may do this, Intuitive-Feeling personalities will find it more natural.

Sensing-Perceiving types, who are marked by an attitude of openness to whatever direction the Spirit leads, may be more comfortable with a Franciscan approach, which ties prayer to acts of loving service. Francis of Assisi himself has been characterized as a "nature mystic" who saw the beauty, goodness, and love of God in everything.[4] *The Canticle of Brother Sun* shows how Francis put a face and a heart on nature.

> All praise be yours, my Lord, through all that you have made,
> > And first my lord Brother Sun,
> > Who brings the day; and light you give to us through him.
> How beautiful is he, how radiant in all his splendour!
> > Of you, Most High, he bears the likeness.
> All praise be yours, my Lord, through Sister Moon and Stars;
> > In the heavens you have made them, bright
> > And precious and fair.
> All praise be yours, my Lord, through Brothers Wind and Air,
> > And fair and stormy, all the weather's moods,
> > By which you cherish all that you have made.

---

3 Cassian *Conferences* 10.11; Library of Christian Classics, XII:244.

4 Edward A. Armstrong, *Saint Francis: Nature Mystic* (Berkeley: University of California Press, 1973), 9.

All praise be yours, my Lord, through Sister Water,
So useful, lowly, precious and pure.
All praise be yours, my Lord, through Brother Fire,
Through whom you brighten up the night,
How beautiful is he, how gay! Full of power and
strength.
All praise be yours, my Lord, through Sister Earth, our
mother,
Who feeds us in her sovereignty and produces
Various fruits with coloured flowers and herbs.[5]

This is not pantheism, but panentheism (the doctrine that God includes the world as a part though not all of God's being). To Francis, "all nature sings and round us rings the music of the spheres." His follower and first biographer, Thomas of Celano, reported,

When he found an abundance of flowers, he preached to them and invited them to praise the Lord as though they were endowed with reason.... Finally, he called all creatures *brother*, and in a most extraordinary manner, a manner never experienced by others, he discerned the hidden things of nature with his sensitive heart, as one who had already escaped *into the freedom of the glory of the sons of God.*[6]

Intuitive-Thinking types may feel more at home with Thomistic prayer, which emphasizes an orderly progression of thought and favors logical, rational, discursive meditation. In this form of prayer one takes a virtue or fault or theological truth and looks at it from every angle. Michael and Norissey

---

[5] Francis of Assisi, *The Canticle of Brother Sun; St. Francis of Assisi: Writings and Early Biographies*, ed. Marion A. Habig (Chicago: Franciscan Herald Press, 1973), 130-31.
[6] Thomas of Celano *First Life* 81, in ibid., 296-97.

recommend using the seven auxiliary questions—what, why, how, who, where, when, and with what helps—and applying them to each question. The danger in this type of prayer is that it may lapse into an impersonal research or study project and neglect emotions and feeling.

All four basic temperaments can benefit from the Benedictine *lectio divina*. The *lectio* entails four steps that correspond to the four basic psychological functions. (1) *Lectio* (reading) employs the *sensing* function in reading and reflecting on scriptures, other writings, other media, nature, people, and so on. (2) *Meditatio* uses the *thinking* function to ruminate on the insights gained through *lectio*. The early monks compared this to a cow chewing the cud. (3) *Oratio* (prayer) personalizes these insights in order to lead one into conversation or communication with God. (4) *Contemplatio* draws on the *intuitive* function to bring the whole process into a coherent whole through immediate awareness of God. Here should occur the union of love that should flow from your dialogue with God. The *lectio divina* is an approach suitable for both beginners and more advanced believers. (For more about *lectio*, see *Gathered in the Word* by Norvene Vest.)

Tilting Toward the Weak Side

For the most part, you will favor the pull exerted by your personality preference. For spiritual growth, however, it is important to favor the weak side. You can develop your inferior function with the help of grace. Certain prayer forms can activate the transcendent dimension of each function. For the *sensing* function—the Franciscan and Ignatian prayer methods with their stress on feeling and imagination. For the *intuitive* function—the Augustinian method that makes much of symbol or sign. For the *thinking* function—the Thomistic method that stresses delving deeply into revealed truths and reconciling opposites. For the *feeling* function—the Augustinian, Franciscan, Ignatian, and Benedictine methods. The key issue is desire. Do you want to become more well rounded in the spiritual life? Or are you content to be carried along by the dominant function?

How important it is to balance experiential, intellectual, social, and institutional dimensions in the spiritual life! The vitality of your spiritual life will depend on strengthening each of these as you respond in your total person to the love of God.

Corporate Worship and Personality Type

With so much attention to personality type you are apt to forget how much regular gathering with a community may contribute to healthy spiritual development. Protestantism, particularly in the United States, has tended to overvalue individual piety and to undervalue corporate. The Enlightenment sent individualism rocketing skyward, and it has gone higher and higher with every generation toward what Charles Reich called "Consciousness III," a hyperindividualism that threatens the very existence of society. That outlook has carried over into the sphere of spirituality as we see a trait among baby boomers and Gen Xers to value spirituality and community but not institutional religion. It is less important to know which aspect of corporate worship satisfies a certain personality trait than to recognize the contribution that corporate worship has always made to the incredibly diverse Body of Christ gathered in every congregation. For that to happen, Grace must transcend the diversities just as it reaches far beyond any limitations set by personality.

Most persons depend on the gathering for worship for their spiritual guidance, and they are not mistaken in expecting it to meet some of their most basic needs. Michael and Norrisey have pointed out the ways that corporate worship covers all of the major personality functions. The community satisfies the *feeling* function, the sermon the *thinking* function, the cross both as symbol and as message the *sensing* function, and the Lord's Supper the *intuitive* function. Whether or not you are part of a worship leadership team, you will find that corporate worship offers the basic foundation for your continuing spiritual journey. Worship God with the Body of Christ, open yourself to God in the private spaces of your life, serve God, and shepherd the people in all that you do.

Selected Bibliography

1. Is Spiritual Formation Needed?

Berry, Carmen Renee, and Mark Lloyd Taylor. *Loving Yourself as Your Neighbor: A Recovery Guide for Christians Escaping Burnout and Codependency.* San Francisco: Harper & Row, 1990.

Bonhoeffer, Dietrich. *Spiritual Care.* Translated by Jay C. Rochelle. Philadelphia, Pa.: Augsburg Fortress Publishers, 1985.

Edwards, Tilden. *Spiritual Friend.: Reclaiming the Gift of Spiritual Direction.* New York: Paulist Press, 1997.

Freeman, Forster. *Readiness for Ministry through Spiritual Direction.* Washington, D.C.: Alban Institute, 1986.

Grenz, Stanley J. *A Primer to Postmodernism.* Grand Rapids, Mich.: Wm. B. Eerdmans Publishing Co., 1996.

Guenther, Margaret. *Holy Listening: The Art of Spiritual Direction.* Boston, Mass.: Cowley Publications, 1992.

Lakeland, Paul. *Postmodernity: Christian Identity in a Fragmented Age.* Minneapolis, Minn.: Augsburg Fortress Publishers, 1997.

Merton, Thomas. *Spiritual Direction and Meditation.* Collegeville, Minn.: Liturgical Press, 1960.

Nemeck, Francis Kelly, and Marie Theresa Coomes. *The Way of Spiritual Direction.* Minneapolis, Minn..: Liturgical Press, 1985.

Oswald, Roy M. Clergy *Self-Care: Finding a Balance for Effective Ministry.* Bethesda, Md.: Alban Institute, 1991.

Peterson, Eugene H. *The Contemplative Pastor: Returning to the Art of*

Spiritual Direction. Grand Rapids, Mich.: Wm. B. Eerdmans Publishing Co., 1993.

Roof, Wade Clark. *A Generation of Seekers: The Spiritual Journeys of the Baby Boom Generation*. San Francisco: HarperSanFrancisco, 1993.

Schuler, David S., Milo L. Brekke, and Merton P. Strommen. *Readiness for Ministry*. Vandalia, Ohio: The Association of Theological Schools in the United States and Canada, 1975.

Yungblut, John R. *The Gentle Art of Spiritual Guidance*. New York: Continuum Publishing Co., 1995.

2. Spiritual Formation of Christian Leaders in History

Clebsch, William A., and Charles R. Jaekle. *Pastoral Care in Historical Perspective*. Northvale, N.J.: Jason Aronson Publishers, 1994.

Hausherr, Irénée. *Spiritual Direction in the Early Easern Church*. Translated by Anthony P. Gythiel. Kalamazoo, Mich.: Cistercian Publications, n.d.

The Ministry in Historical Perspectives. Edited by H. Richard Niebuhr and Daniel Day Williams. San Francisco: Harper & Row, 1956, 1983.

Sage, Athanase. *The Religious Life According to St. Augustine*. Translated by Paul C. Thabault. Brooklyn: New City Press, 1990.

Spener, Philip Jacob. *Pia Desideria*. Translated and edited by Theodore G. Tappert. Philadelphia, Pa.: Augsburg Fortress Publishers, 1964.

Thornton, Edward R. *Professional Education for Ministry: A History of Clinical Pastoral Education*. Nashville: Abingdon Press, 1970.

Writings on Spiritual Direction by Great Christian Masters. Edited by Jerome M. Venfelder and Mary C. Coelho. New York: Seabury Press, 1982.

3. The Main Thing: A Relationship with God

The Art of Prayer: An Orthodox Anthology. Compiled by Igumen Chariton of Valamo. London: Faber & Faber, Inc., 1997.

Baillie, John. *Christian Devotion*. New York: Charles Scribner's Sons, 1962, especially pp. 43–51.

_____. *A Diary of Private Prayer*. New York: Simon & Schuster Trade, 1996.

Balthasar, Hans Urs von. *Prayer*. Translated by Graham Harrison.. San Francisco, Calif.: Ignatius Press, 1986.

Barth, Karl. *Prayer*. 2d ed. Edited by Don E. Saliers. Philadelphia: Westminster Press, 1985.

Bondi, Roberta C. *In Ordinary Time: Healing the Wounds of the Heart*. Nashville, Tenn.: Abingdon Press, 1996.

_____. *Memories of God: Theological Reflections on Life*. Nashville, Tenn.: Abingdon Press, 1995.

_____. *To Pray and to Love: Conversations on Prayer with the Early Church.* Minneapolis, Minn.: Augsburg Fortress Publishers, 1991.

Bonhoeffer, Dietrich. *Prayers from Prison.* Interpreted by Christoph Hempe. London: Collins, 1977.

Bounds, E.M. *Power through Prayer.* New Kensington, Pa.: Whitaker House, n.d. *Prayer and Praying Men.* Ada, Mich.: Baker Books, 1992.

Bowden, Guy A. *The Dazzling Darkness: An Essay on the Experience of Prayer.* London: SPCK, 1963.

Brémond, Henri. *Prayer and Poetry.* Translated by Algar Thorold. London: Burns, Oates & Washbourne, 1927.

Brooke, Avery. *Learning and Teaching Christian Meditation.* Rev. ed. Cambridge, Mass.: Cowley Publications, 1990.

Buttrick, George A. *Prayer.* New York and Nashville: Abingdon-Cokesbury, 1942.

Carter, Harold A. *The Prayer Tradition of Black People.* Valley Forge, Pa.: Judson Press,1976.

Carver, William Owen. *Thou When Thou Prayest.* Nashville: Sunday School Board, SBC, 1928.

Clemmons, William. *Discovering the Depths.* Nashville: Broadman Press, 1976.

Coburn, John B. *A Life to Live—A Way to Pray.* New York: Seabury Press, 1973. _____. *Prayer and Personal Religion.* New York: Walker Publishing Co., 1985.

Daly, Gabriel, O.S.A. *Asking the Father: A Study of the Prayer of Petition.* Ways of Prayer Series. Wilmington, Del.: Michael Glazier, 1982.

Daujat, Jean. *Prayer.* Translated by Martin Murphy. New York: Hawthorn Books, 1964.

DelBene, Ron. *The Hunger of the Heart: A Call to Spiritual Growth.* Nashville, Tenn.: Upper Room Books, 1992.

Duquoc, Christian, and Claude Geffré, eds. *The Prayer Life.* Concilium, vol. 79. New York: Herder & Herder, 1972.

Ellul, Jacques. *Prayer and Modern Man.* Translated by G. Edward Hopkin. New York: Seabury Press, 1970.

Farmer, Herbert H. *The World and God: A Study of Prayer, Providence and Miracle in Christian Experience.* London: Nisbet & Co., 1948.

Forsyth, Peter Taylor. *The Soul of Prayer.* Bellingham, Wash.: Regent College Publishing, 1993..

Fosdick, Harry E. *The Meaning of Prayer.* Minneapolis, Minn.: Macalester Park Publishing, 1997.

Gallen, John, ed. *Christians at Prayer.* Notre Dame, Ind.: University of Notre Dame Press, 1976.

Garrett, Constance. *Growth in Prayer*. New York: Macmillan, 1950.

Gibbard, Mark. *Guides to Hidden Springs*. London: SCM Press, 1979.

_____. *Prayer and Contemplation*. London: Mowbrays, 1976.

_____. *Twelve Who Prayed*. Minneapolis: Augsburg, 1977.

_____. *Why Pray?* London: SCM Press, 1970.

Gossip, Arthur John. *In the Secret Place of the Most High*. New York: Charles Scribner's Sons, 1947.

Groff, Warren F. *Prayer: God's Time and Ours!* Ann Arbor, Mich.: Books on Demand, 1984.

Hallesby, Ole Christian. *Prayer*. Minneapolis, Minn.: Augsburg Fortress Publishers, 1994.

Hallock, Edgar F. *Prayer and Meditation*. Nashville: Broadman Press, 1940.

Harkness, Georgia. *Prayer and the Common Life*. New York: Abingdon-Cokesbury, 1948.

_____. *The Religious Life*. New York: Association Press, 1953.

Harrington, Wilfrid, O.P. *Prodigal Father*. Ways of Prayer, 2. Wilmington, Del.: Michael Glazier, 1982.

Hausherr, Irénée. *The Name of Jesus*. Translated by Charles Cummings. Kalamazoo, Mich.: Cistercian Publications, 1978.

Hazelton, Roger. *The Root and Flower of Prayer*. New York: Macmillan, 1943.

Heard, Gerald. *A Preface to Prayer*. New York and London: Harper & Brothers, 1944.

Higgins, John J. *Merton's Theology of Prayer*. Spencer, Mass.: Cistercian Publications, 1971.

Hinson, E. Glenn. *The Reaffirmation of Prayer*. Nashville: Broadman Press, 1979.

_____. *A Serious Call to a Contemplative Lifestyle*. Rev. ed. Macon, Ga.: Smyth & Helwys, 1993.

Irwin, Kevin. *Liturgy, Prayer and Spirituality*. New York: Paulist Press, 1984.

John XXIII, Pope. *Prayers and Devotions of Pope John XXIII*. Edited by John P. Donnelly. London: Burns & Oates, 1967.

Jones, Rufus M. *The Double Search: Studies in Atonement and Prayer*. Philadelphia: John C. Winston Co., 1906.

_____. "What Does Prayer Mean?" *In Rufus Jones Speaks to Our Time*, edited by Harry Emerson Fosdick. New York: Macmillan, 1957.

Kelsey, Morton. *The Other Side of Silence: Meditation for the Twenty-First Century*. New York: Paulist Press, 1997.

Klenicki, Leon, and Gabe Huck, eds. *Spirituality and Prayer: Jewish and Christian Understandings*. Ann Arbor, Mich.: Books on Demand, n.d.

Laubach, Frank Charles. *Frank Laubach's Prayer Diary*. Westwood, N.J.: Revell, 1964.

Leech, Kenneth. *True Prayer: An Invitation to Christian Spirituality.* Harrisburg, Pa.: Morehouse Publishing, 1995.

LeFevre, Perry. *Understandings of Prayer.* Philadelphia: Westminster Press, 1981.

Lewis, C. S. *Letters to Malcolm: Chiefly on Prayer.* New York: Harcourt, Brace & Company, 1972.

McEachern, Alton H. *A Pattern of Prayer.* Nashville: J. M. Productions, 1982.

Macy, Howard R. *Rhythms of the Inner Life.* Newbery, Ore.: Barclay Press, 1992.

Maloney, George, S.J. *Centering on the Lord Jesus.* Ways of Prayer, 3. Wilmington, Del.: Michael Glazier, 1982.

Mangan, Celine, O.P. *Can We Still Call God "Father"?* Ways of Prayer, 12. Wilmington, Del.: Michael Glazier, 1984.

Merton, Thomas. *Contemplative Prayer.* NewYork: Doubleday Image Books, 1971.

_____. *New Seeds of Contemplation.* New York: New Directions Publishing, 1972.

Northcott, Hubert. *The Venture of Prayer.* London: SPCK, 1962.

Oates, Wayne E. *Nurturing Silence in a Noisy Hear: How to Find Inner Peace.* Minneapolis, Minn.: Augsburg Fortress Publishers, 1996.

O'Driscoll, Herbert. *A Doorway in Time.* San Francisco: Harper & Row, 1985.

Osiek, Carolyn, and Donald Senior, eds. *Scripture and Prayer.* Wilmington, Del.: Michael Glazier, 1988.

Paterson, William F. *The Power of Prayer.* New York: Macmillan, 1970.

Pennington, Basil, O.C.S.O. *Centering Prayer: Renewing an Ancient Christian Prayer Form.* New York: Doubleday & Co., 1982.

_____. *Challenges in Prayer.* Ways of Prayer, l. Wilmington, Del.: Michael Glazier, 1982.

_____. *The Way Back Home: An Introduction to Centering Prayer.* New York: Paulist Press, 1982.

Pittenger, William Norman. *God's Way with Men: A Study of the Relationship between God and Man in Providence, "Miracle," and Prayer.* London: Hodder & Stoughton, 1969.

Poling, David A. *Faith Is Power for You.* New York: Greenberg, 1950.

Porteous, John. *Order and Grace: A Discussion of Prayer, Providence, and Miracle.* London: James Clarke, 1925.

Puglisi, Pico Mario. *Prayer.* Translated by Bernard M. Allen. New York: Macmillan, 1929.

Quoist, Michel. *Prayers.* Translated by Agnes M. Forsyth and Anne Marie de Commaile. Franklin, Wis.: Sheed & Ward, 1985.

Raguin, Yves. *How to Pray Today*. Translated by John Beevers. St. Meinrad, Ind.: Abbey Press, 1974.

Rauschenbusch, Walter. *Prayers of the Social Awakening*. Fresno, Calif.: Kairos World Press, 1996.

Rhymes, Douglas. *Prayer in the Secular City*. Philadelphia: Westminster Press, 1967.

_____. *Through Prayer to Reality*. Winona, Minn.: St. Mary's College Press, 1974.

Roberts, Howard. *Learning to Pray*. Nashville: Broadman Press, 1984.

Schmidt, Herman, ed. *Prayer and Community*. Concilium, vol. 52. New York: Herder & Herder, 1970.

Steere, Douglas V. *Dimensions of Prayer: Cultivating a Relationship with God*, revised edition. Nashville, Tenn.: Upper Room Books, 1997.

_____. *On Listening to Another*. New York: Harper & Brothers, 1955.

_____. *Prayer and Worship*. New York: Association Press, 1938.

_____. *Prayer in the Contemporary World*. Wallingford, Penn.: Pendle Hill Publications, 1990..

_____. *Work and Contemplation*. New York: Harper & Brothers, 1957.

Stoddart, Jane T. *Private Prayer in Christian Story*. Garden City, N.Y.: Doubleday, Doran, 1928.

Teilhard de Chardin, Pierre. *The Divine Milieu: An Essay on the Interior Life*. New York: HarperCollins, 1975.

Underhill, Evelyn. *The Golden Sequence: A Fourfold Study of the Spiritual Life*. New York: E. P. Dutton, 1933.

_____. *The Life of the Spirit and the Life of Today*. Harrisburg, Pa.: Morehouse Publishing, 1995.

_____. *Mysticism: The Nature and Development of Spiritual Consciousness*. Boston, Mass.: OneWorld Publications, 1994.

Vischer, Lukas. *Intercession*. Geneva: World Council of Churches, 1980.

_____. *The Way of the Pilgrim*. Translated by R. M. French. New York: Ballantine, 1974.

Whiston, Charles F. *Pray: A Study of Distinctively Christian Praying*. Grand Rapids: Eerdmans, 1972.

_____. *Teach Us to Pray*. Boston: Pilgrim Press, 1949.

_____. *When Ye Pray, Say Our Father*. Boston: Pilgrim Press, 1960.

Winward, Stephen F. *Teach Yourself to Pray*. New York: Harper & Row, 1961.

4. Holding Yourself Accountable

Baldwin, Christina. *One to One: Self-Understanding Through Journal Writing*. New York: M. Evans & Company, 1991.

Kelsey, Morton T. *Adventure Inward: Christian Growth through Personal Journal Writing.* Minneapolis, Minn.: Augsburg Fortress Publishers, 1980.

Lindbergh, Anne Morrow. *Gift from the Sea.* New York: Vintage Books, 1991.

Progroff, Ira. *At a Journal Workshop: Writing to Access the Power of the Unconscious and Evoke Creative Ability.* New York: Putnam Publishing, 1992 (2nd edition).

_____. *The Practice of Process Meditation: The Intensive Journal Way to Spiritual Experience.* New York: Dialogue House Library, 1980.

Roh, Ray. *Keeping a Spiritual Journal.* Pecos, N.Mex.: Dove Publishing, 1978.

Simons, George F. *Keeping Your Personal Journal.* New York: Paulist Press, 1978.

5. Making the Most of Your Time

Blizzard, Samuel W. *The Protestant Parish Minister: A Behavioral Science Interpretation.* Monograph Series No. 5. West Lafayette, Ind.: Society for the Scientific Study of Religion, 1985.

Caussade, Jean-Pierre de. *The Sacrament of the Present Moment.* Translated by Kitty Muggeridge. San Francisco: HarperSanFrancisco, 1989.

Cullmann, Oscar. *Christ and Time: The Primitive Conception of Time and History.* New York: Gordon Press Publishers, 1977.

Edwards, Tilden. *Living in the Presence: Spiritual Exercises to Open Our Lives to the Awareness of God.* San Francisco: Harper SanFrancisco, 1995.

_____. *Living Simply Through the Day: Spiritual Survival in a Complex Age.* New York: Paulist Press, 1977.

_____. *Sabbath Time: Understanding and Practice for Contemporary Christians.* Rev. ed. Nashville: Upper Room Books, 1992.

Kelly, Thomas R. *A Testament of Devotion.* San Francisco: Harper SanFrancisco, 1996.

Oates, Wayne E. *Confessions of a Workaholic.* New York: World Publishing, 1971.

6. Maintaining Balance

Augustine. *Confessions.* Translated by John K. Ryan. New York: Image Books, 1960.

_____. *Soliloquies* NPNF, Series 1, VII:539.

Bernard of Clairvaux *Sermon 74 on the Song of Songs* 5-6, in *Varieties of Mystic Experience* by Elmer O'Brien, S.J. (New York: Mentor-Omega Book, 1964), 105.

Bernard of Clairvaux. *Sermon 84 on the Song of Songs* 2; Library of Christian Classics.

Catherine of Siena. *The Dialogue*. Translated by Suzanne Noffke, O.P. Classics of Western Spirituality. New York: Paulist Press, 1980.

Dumont, Charles "A Contemplative at the Heart of the World: Thomas Merton," *Lumen* 24 :1969.

Forest, James. "The Gift of Merton," *Commonweal*, January 10, 1969.

Hammarskjöld, Dag. *Markings*. Translated by Leif Sjöberg and W. H. Auden. London: Faber and Faber, 1964.

Heschel, Abraham Joshua. *Man Is Not Alone: A Philosophy of Religion*. New York: Farrar, Straus & Giroux, 1951.

Hilton, Walter. *The Stairway of Perfection*. Translated by M. L. Del Mastro. New York: Image Books, 1979.

Hinson, E. Glenn "Contemptus Mundi-Amor Mundi: Merton's Progression from World Denial to World Affirmation," *Cistercian Studies* 26:1991.

_____. *Love at the Heart of Things*. Wallingford, Pa.: Pendle Hill, 1998.

_____. "The Catholicizing of Contemplation: Thomas Merton's Place in the Church's Prayer Life." *Perspectives in Religious Studies* 1: 1974.

Hugo of St. Victor. *Nineteen Sermons on Ecclesiastes*: Library of Christian Classics in *Late Medieval Mysticism*. Edited by Ray C. Petry. Philadelphia: Westminister Press, 1957.

Jones, Rufus M. *The Double Search: Studies in Atonement and Prayer*. Philadelphia: J. C. Winston, 1906.

Kelly, Thomas R. *A Testament of Devotion*. New York: Harper and Row, 1941.

Leclercq, O.S.B., Jean. *The Love of Learning and the Desire for God: A Study of Monastic Culture*. Translated by Catharine Misrahi. New York: Fordham University Press, 1961.

McGinn, Bernard. *The Growth of Mysticism: From Gregory the Great Through the 12th Century*. New York: Crossroad Herder, 1996.

Merton, Thomas. *A Vow of Conversation: Journals 1964-1965*. New York: Farrar, Straus, & Giroux, 1988.

Merton, Thomas. *Conjectures of a Guilty Bystander*. New York: Image Books, 1968.

Merton, Thomas. *No Man Is an Island*. New York: Harcourt, Brace, and Jovanovich, 1955.

Merton, Thomas. *The Sign of Jonas*. New York: Harcourt, Brace, & Giroux, 1979.

Pascal, Blaise. *Pensées*. Edited by Louis Lafuma. Translated by John Warrington. London: J. M. Dent & Sons; New York: E. P. Dutton, 1960.

Robinson, John A. T. *Honest to God*. London: SCM Press; Philadelphia: Westminster Press, 1963.

Schultenover, David G. *George Tyrrell in Search of Catholicism*. Shepherdstown, Penn.: Patmos Press, 1981.

Steere, Douglas V. *On Speaking Out of the Silence*. Wallingford, Penn.: Pendle Hill Publications, 1972.

_____. *Classics of Western Spirituality*. New York: Paulist Press, 1984.

_____. *The Open Life*. Philadelphia, Penn.: Book Committee of the Religious Society of Friends, 1937.

Teilhard de Chardin, Pierre. *Le Milieu Divin*. London: Fontana Books, 1962.

Woolman, John *The Journal of John Woolman*. New York: Corinth Books, 1961.

7. Sexuality and Spirituality

Kelsey, Morton T., and Barbara Kelsey. *Sacrament of Sexuality: The Spirituality and Psychology of Sex*. Warwick, N.Y.: Amity House, 1986.

Moore, John. *Sexuality, Spirituality: A Study of Feminine/Masculine Relationship*. Tisbury, Wiltshire, England: Element Books, 1980.

Morrison, Melanie. *The Grace of Coming Home: Spirituality, Sexuality, and the Struggle for Justice*. Cleveland, Ohio: Pilgrim Press, 1995.

Nelson, James B. *The Intimate Connection: Male Sexuality, Masculine Spirituality*. Philadelphia: Westminster John Knox Press, 1988.

Timmerman, Joan H. *Sexuality and Spiritual Growth*. New York: Crossroad, 1992.

8. Spiritual Reading, Listening, and Seeing

Armstrong, Edward A. *Saint Francis: Nature Mystic: The Derivation and Significance of the Nature Stories in the Franciscan Legend*. Ann Arbor, Mich.: Books on Demand, n.d.

Baggley, John and Richard Temple. *Doors of Perception: Icons and Their Spiritual Significance*. Crestwood, N.Y.: St. Vladimir's Seminary Press, 1988.

Chittister, Joan D. *A Passion for Life: Fragments of the Face of God*. Maryknoll, N.Y.: Orbis Books, 1996.

Christian Spirituality. Edited by Frank N. Magill and Ian P. McGreal. San Francisco: Harper & Row, 1988.

Forest, James H. *Praying with Icons*. Maryknoll, N.Y.: Orbis Books, 1997.

Galavaris, George. *The Icon in the Life of the Church: Doctrine, Liturgy, Devotion*. Leiden: E. J. Brill, 1981.

Hinson, E. Glenn. *Seekers after Mature Faith*. Waco, Tex.: Word Books, 1968.

L'Engle, Madeleine. *Penguins + Golden Calves: Icons and Idols*. Wheaton, Ill.: Harold Shaw, Publishers, 1996.

Limouris, Gennadios. *Icons: Windows on Eternity*. Faith and Order Paper 147. Geneva: World Council of Churches Publications, 1990.

Mogabgab, John. "Along the Desert Road: Notes on Spiritual Reading." In
Spirituality in Ecumenical Perspective, edited by E. Glenn Hinson.
Louisville: Westminster/John Knox Press, 1993.

Nouwen, Henri J. M. *Behold the Beauty of the Lord: Praying with Icons*. Notre
Dame, Ind.: Ave Maria Press, 1987.

Ouspensky, Leonide, and Vladimir Lossky. *The Meaning of Icons*. Translated
by G. E. H. Palmer and E. Kadloubovsky. Rev. ed. Crestwood, N.Y.: St.
Vladimir's Seminary Press, 1982.

Pelikan, Jaroslav Jan. *Imago Dei: The Byzantine Apologia for Icons*.
Washington, D.C.: National Gallery of Art; Princeton, N.J.: Princeton
University Press, 1990.

Quenot, Michel. *The Icon: Window on the Kingdom*. Crestwood, N.Y.: St.
Vladimir's Seminary Press, 1991.

Steere, Douglas V. *Doors into Life through Five Devotional Classics*. New
York: Harper & Row, 1948.

9. Seeking Solitude and Silence

DelBene, Ron. *Alone with God: A Guide for Personal Retreats*. Nashville,
Tenn.: Upper Room Books, 1997.

Griffin, Emilie. *Wilderness Time: A Guide to Spiritual Retreat*. San Francisco:
Harper SanFrancisco, 1997.

Hart, Thomas N. *Coming Down the Mountain: How to Turn Your Retreat into
Everyday Living*. New York: Paulist Press, 1988.

Job, Rueben P. *A Guide to Retreat for All God's Shepherds*. Nashville, Tenn.:
Abingdon Press, 1994.

Maloney, George A. *An Eight-day Retreat: Alone with the Alone*. Notre Dame,
Ind.: Ave Maria Press, 1982.

Nelson, Virgil. *Retreat Handbook: A Way to Meaning*. Valley Forge, Pa.:
Judson Press, 1976.

Padovano, Anthony T. *A Retreat with Thomas Merton: Becoming Who We Are*.
Cincinnati, Ohio: St. Anthony Messenger Press, 1995.

Pennington, M. Basil. *A Retreat with Thomas Merton*. New York: Continuum
Publishing Co., 1995.

Shawchuck, Norman, Rueben P. Job, and Robert G. Doherty. *How to Conduct
a Spiritual Life Retreat*. Nashville: The Upper Room, 1986.

Steere, Douglas V. *Time to Spare*. New York: Harper Brothers, 1949.

Studdert-Kennedy, Geoffrey A. *The New Man in Christ*. Edited by the Dean of
Worcester. London: Hodder & Stoughton, 1932.

Underhill, Evelyn. *The Fruits of the Spirit*. Harrisburg, Penn.: Morehouse
Publishing, 1989.

_____. *The Ways of the Spirit.* Edited by Grace A. Brame. New York: Crossroad, 1990.

10. Sharing the Journey

Allen, Joseph J. *Inner Way: Toward a Rebirth of Eastern Christian Spiritual Direction.* Grand Rapids, Mich.: Wm. B. Eerdmans Publishing Co., 1994.

Barry, William A. *Spiritual Direction and the Encounter with God: A Theological Inquiry.* New York: Paulist Press, 1992.

Barry, William A., and William J. Connolly. *The Practice of Spiritual Direction.* New York: Seabury Press, 1982.

Bonhoeffer, Dietrich. *Spiritual Care.* Translated by Jay C. Rochelle. Philadelphia, Penn.: Augsburg Fortress Press, 1985.

Boyer, Ernest, Jr. *A Way in the World: Family Life as Spiritual Discipline.* San Francisco: Harper & Row, 1987.

Common Journey, Different Paths: Spiritual Direction in Cross-Cultural Perspective. Edited by Susan Rakoczy. Maryknoll, N.Y.: Orbis, 1992.

Culligan, Kevin. *Spiritual Direction: Contemporary Readings.* New York: Living Flame, 1983.

Dougherty, Rose Mary, S.S.N.D. *Group Spiritual Direction: Community for Discernment.* Mahwah, N.J.: Paulist Press, 1995.

Dyckman, Katherine Marie and L. Patrick Carroll. *Inviting the Mystic, Supporting the Prophet: An Introduction to Spiritual Direction.* Mahwah, N.J.: Paulist Press, 1981.

Edwards, Tilden. *Spiritual Friend.* New York: Paulist Press, 1980.

Fischer, Kathleen R. *Women at the Well: Feminist Perspectives on Spiritual Direction.* New York: Paulist Press, 1988.

Freeman, Forster. *Readiness for Ministry through Spiritual Direction.* Washington, D.C.: Alban Institute, 1986.

Gratton, Carolyn. *The Art of Spiritual Guidance: A Contemporary Approach to Growing in the Spirit.* New York: Crossroad, 1993.

Groff, Kent Ira. *Active Spirituality: A Guide for Seekers and Ministers.* Bethesda, Md.: Alban Institute, 1993.

Grosh, Gerald R. *Quest for Sanctity.* Wilmington, Del.: Michael Glazier, 1988.

Guenther, Margaret. *Holy Listening: The Art of Spiritual Direction.* Cambridge, Mass.: Cowley Publications, 1992.

Johnson, Ben Campbell. *Speaking of God: Evangelism as Initial Spiritual Guidance.* Louisville: Westminster John Knox, 1991.

Jones, Alan W. *Exploring Spiritual Direction: An Essay in Christian Friendship.* New York: Seabury Press, 1982.

Kelsey, Morton T. *Companions on the Inner Way: The Art of Spiritual Direction.* New York: Crossroad, 1983.

_____. *Set Your Hearts on the Greatest Gift: Living the Art of Christian Love.* Hyde Park, N.Y.: New City Press, 1996 and Nashville, Tenn.: Upper Room Books, 1996.

Laplace, Jean. *Preparing for Spiritual Direction.* Translated by John C. Guinness. Chicago: Franciscan Herald Press, 1975.

Leckey, Dolores. *Growing in the Spirit.* Washington, D.C.: Alban Institute, 1975.

Leech, Kenneth. *Soul Friend: An Invitation to Spiritual Direction.* San Francisco: HarperSanFrancisco, 1992.

_____. *Spirituality and Pastoral Care.* Cambridge, Mass.: Cowley Publications, 1989.

Merton, Thomas. *The School of Charity: The Letters of Thomas Merton on Religious Renewal and Spiritual Direction.* Edited by Patrick Hart. New York: Farrar, Straus, & Giroux, 1990.

_____. *Spiritual Direction and Meditation.* Collegeville, Minn.: Liturgical Press, 1960.

Morneau, Robert F. *Spiritual Direction: Principles and Practices.* New York: Crossroad, 1992.

Nemeck, Francis Kelly, and Marie Theresa Coomes. *The Way of Spiritual Direction.* Wilmington, Del.: Michael Glazier, 1985.

Peterson, Eugene H. *The Contemplative Pastor: Returning to the Art of Spiritual Direction.* Grand Rapids: Eerdmans, 1993.

Rohr, Richard. *Spiritual Direction and Growth within the Family.* Kansas City, Mo.: National Catholic Reporter, 1988.

Ruffing, Janet. *Uncovering Stories of Faith: Spiritual Direction and Narrative.* New York: Paulist Press, 1989.

Sellner, Edward Cletus. *Mentoring: The Ministry of Spiritual Kinship.* Notre Dame, Ind.: Ave Maria Press, 1990.

Spiritual Direction: Contemporary Readings. Edited by Kevin G. Culligan. Locust Valley, N.Y.: Living Flame, 1983.

Studzinski, Raymond. *Spiritual Direction and Midlife Development.* Chicago: Loyola University, 1985.

Thornton, Martin. *Spiritual Direction.* Cambridge, Mass.: Cowley Publications, 1984

Vanderwall, Francis W. *Spiritual Direction: An Invitation to Abundant Life.* New York: Paulist Press, 1981.

Van Kaam, Adrian L. *Dynamics of Spiritual Direction.* Denville, N.J.: Dimension Books, 1978.

Yungblut, John R. *The Gentle Art of Spiritual Guidance.* New York: Continuum, 1995.

11. What the World and the Church Need Most

Brother Francis: *An Anthology of Writings by and about St. Francis of Assisi.* Edited by Lawrence Cunningham. New York: Harper & Row, 1972.

Egan, Eileen. *Such a Vision of the Street: Mother Teresa—The Spirit and the Work.* New York: Doubleday, 1985.

Francis of Assisi Today. Edited by Christian Duquoc and Floristan Casiano. San Francisco: HarperSanFrancisco, 1981.

My Life for the Poor. Edited by José Luis González-Balado and Janet N. Playfoot. New York: Ballantine, 1987.

Steere, Douglas V. *On Beginning from Within.* New York: Harper Brothers, 1943.

Appendix: Personality and Spirituality

Bryant, Christopher. *Prayer and Different Types of People.* Gainesville, Fla.: Center for Application of Psychological Type, 1983.

Jung, Carl Gustav. *Psychological Types.* Princeton, N.J.: Princeton University Press, 1959.

Keating, Charles J. *Who We Are Is How We Pray: Matching Personality and Spirituality.* Mystic, Conn.: Twenty-third Publications, 1987.

Michael, Chester P., and Marie C. Norrisey. *Prayer and Temperament: Different Prayer Forms for Different Personality Types.* Charlottesville, Va.: Open Door, 1984.

Myers, Isabel Briggs, and Peter Myers. *Gifts Differing.* Palo Alto, Calif.: Consulting Psychologists Press, 1980.

About the Author

E. Glenn Hinson retired as Professor of Spirituality and John Loftis Professor of Church History at Baptist Theological Seminary at Richmond. Dr. Hinson also taught at Catholic University, Wake Forest University, and Southern Seminary in Louisville. He has received fellowships from the Association of Theological Schools. Academic honors include the Johannes Quasten Medal for Excellence in Religious Studies at Catholic University and the Cuthbert Allen Memorial Award given by Wake Forest University and Belmont Abbey.

Dr. Hinson earned degrees from Washington University (B.A.), Southern Seminary (B.D., Th.D.), and Oxford University (D.Phil.). Hinson focused on Patristics at Oxford. Key influences in spirituality for Hinson are Thomas Merton and Douglas Steere. Both of these 20th century writers guide Hinson's thought in this volume.

Hinson is on the Advisory Board of Weavings: A Journal of Christian Spirituality and is on the faculty of the Academy for Spiritual Formation, both part of The Upper Room Ministries. He is also a member of numerous professional organizations, including the American Society of Church History and the American Academy of Religion.

He lives in Louisville, Kentucky. Hinson guides retreats, lectures, and preaches around the world.